God's Vitamin "C" for the Spirit™ of WOMEN

Compiled by Kathy Collard Miller

P. O. Box 4123, Lancaster, Pennsylvania 17604

Kathy Collard Miller is the author of twenty-five books, including the best-sellers, *God's Vitamin "C" for the Spirit* and *God's Chewable Vitamin "C" for the Spirit.* She has written for *The Christian Communicator, Moody Monthly, L A Times,* and *Today's Christian Woman.* Kathy speaks regularly and has appeared on many talk shows including the *700 club.* She lives in Placentia, California with her husband Larry.

She can be reached for scheduling speaking engagements at P. O. Box 1058, Placentia, California 92871 (714) 993-2654.

To schedule Author appearances write:
Author Appearances, Starburst Promotions, P. O. Box 4123
Lancaster, Pennsylvania 17604 or call (717) 293-0939

Credits:
Cover by David Marty Design
Unless otherwise noted, or paraphrased by the author, all Scripture quotations are from the *King James Version* of The Holy Bible.

GOD'S VITAMIN "C" FOR THE SPIRIT OF WOMEN

ISBN: 1-56865-336-0

Printed in the United States of America

Table of Contents

God's Vitamin "C" for the Spirit of WOMEN is a collection of inspirational Stories, Quotes, Cartoons, and Scriptures by many of your favorite female Christian speakers and writers. It will inspire and delight your spirit. You will find it to be both heart-tugging and thought-provoking.

1

Angels

Do not neglect to show hospitality to strangers, for by this some have entertained angels without knowing it.

Hebrews 13:2

Silent Memories

Grandma was special in so many ways, always happy and smiling and matter-of-fact about everything. I never heard her complain, even though her hands were badly crippled by arthritis and she was left a widow as a young woman to raise two little girls alone.

Chris, Peg, Mom, Dad and I lived with Grandma. Unlike so many families who found it a detriment to have the dreaded mother-in-law around, we were truly blessed by her presence. She was a very wise person, fun to be with and had a beautiful faith in her Lord and Savior. I remember fondly the many Sunday afternoon rides in the country, the picnics under the trees, and all the other things our family did together that Grandma was so much a part of. But I believe the thing I treasure most is Peg and I scrambling into her huge four-poster bed with her, cuddling close and hearing her read to us.

As the years continued, Grandma came down less and less from her room in the corner of the house and became more deaf with each passing day. Since we couldn't afford a hearing aid, we used an ear trumpet (It worked on the same principle as a megaphone, only backwards).

I can still see Peg climbing onto her bed and yelling "I love you, Grandma," at the top of her lungs into that old ear trumpet, and Grandma's soft blue eyes glistening with love, as she would gather Peg into her arms. Toward the end Grandma became completely deaf, but that never stopped Peg from telling her she loved her, or Grandma from smiling. In her silent world she never doubted our love for her, or the love of her Savior.

I was ten when Grandma went to be with Jesus. I remember the day well. It was a sad day for all, but it was brightened when Dad told us that as Grandma drew her last breath a smile crossed her tired, wrinkled face and she whispered, "I hear the birds, oh, listen, hear the birds."

Today, as an adult, when I hear a bird singing sweetly, I smile a secret smile, for I am reminded of a very special person who taught me faith through her silent world of love.

—Marcia Krugh Leaser

The Prayer Partner

It was a beautiful, crisp fall day in Albuquerque, New Mexico. I was busy with last minute chores, waiting for my friend Harriet to stop by for a casual (or so I thought) visit. Soon the doorbell rang, and I welcomed my friend into the house, happy to see her after several months. Soon we were seated at my dining room table, enjoying a cup of coffee.

I began with my usual list of complaints: about life, and my failing marriage. Eventually, I gave Harriet the opportunity to talk. She began by lovingly sharing a little booklet with me that explained the Gospel in simple terms. I listened intently. Within 15 minutes I responded by asking Christ to come into my life and be my Savior. Immediately, I felt something change deep inside me. I was a different person.

My husband noticed a change in me. My attitude was different and my treatment of him was *totally* different. He saw a woman filled with a new love for him and our two precious children. After a couple of meetings with a young seminary student, my husband began longing for the relationship with Christ he had known as a young teenager. One evening he prayed with the student, recommitting his life to the Savior. His prayer included asking God to change our priorities and, especially, our broken relationship.

As our lives began to change, it was difficult to imagine the road we'd traveled the previous seven years of marriage. Our wedding day had taken place in a bare, dim chapel, with less than enthusiastic relatives in attendance. We were two eighteen-year-old kids, expecting a baby. We began living in a one room apartment one block from the local University where my husband was a student. I worked as a typist for minimum wage, trying to save every dime to pay for the baby. Our son soon arrived, bringing with him the added responsibility of parenthood and more pressure to survive. We had one goal in mind: graduate from college, get a great job, and make lots of money so we could be happy.

Four years later, our goal in clear view, we separated. Life was hard, we were disillusioned with marriage and constant unhappiness. To make matters worse, we were expecting a second child. Divorce seemed the only real answer. But right before our daughter was born we decided to give our marriage one more chance. Two years later we were still miserable . . . until Harriet made her visit.

Several months after my conversion, we were transferred to Texas for my husband's job promotion. Both of us felt it was a chance to start over. We quickly became involved in a wonderful church, making sure no one knew about our hurtful past. We didn't want to look back.

In the fall of that same year our new church had a "spiritual renewal" weekend. People came from all over Texas to share of God's faithfulness, healed marriages and hope. We were inspired. We weren't the only people with problems!

At the close of this wonderful weekend we were encouraged to pray together as a couple. As we stepped into the beautiful sanctuary, we noticed that all of the lights were out except the spotlight shining on the huge cross hanging over the choir loft. It was *so* quiet! As we knelt to pray, a gentleman came up behind us, knelt between us and put his arms around our shoulders. He began to pray about *all* our secrets—areas of shame and pain in our marriage, our children, and our future. He finished by encouraging us to lay every need at the foot of the cross, and trust God with it all! He asked the Holy Spirit to guide us, and fill our lives with His love so we could live in victory. I will never forget his assurance that our lives together were going to be all right, our future secure in Christ.

"How does he know so much about us?" we wondered. "We didn't share any of that at the conference!"

We stood to thank him for his wonderful prayer (and see who he was) but *no one* was there . . . the darkened sanctuary was completely empty and silent.

This year we celebrate, with great joy and thankfulness, 35 years of marriage . . . an answer to our prayers, and those of our Prayer Partner.

—Judy Hampton

* Angels From A Three-Year-Old's Perspective

One day when my son was three years old, and restfully napping, I untypically flipped through the afternoon television talk shows. One captured my interest.

A discussion was in progress with adults who, as children, had near-death experiences. I was interested because our son had become very ill at birth, and spent a week on a respirator, two more weeks in intensive care, and six months on oxygen. He made a sudden and incredible recovery at the end of the six months, and was considered "the miracle baby" by members of our immediate family and church families across the country who had been praying for him.

As my attention became fixed upon the discussion of those on television, I suddenly became skeptical when the discussion swayed to "guardian angels." I had heard of them before, but believed they were a "trendy" pursuit of comfort for the human spirit, I would not be easily convinced. Nonetheless, I continued lending a sympathetic ear, and at the end of the show flipped the television off without any further contemplation on the matter.

About a month later, as my son was awakening from a nap, we were playing with the stuffed animals that had been given to him as a newborn in the hospital. We talked about how nice everyone had been to give him these gifts. He said, "I liked the doctors and nurses." I told him how these people had taken good care of him. Then he said, "I liked the one with the fairy wings."

I gasped. My mind immediately flashed back to the television talk show. I was in disbelief. Then to be sure, I asked my son, "Don't you mean the doctors and nurses?" He answered very matter-of-factly, "The lady with the fairy wings was really nice."

To this day, I am a believer of those wonderful angels. When it is out of the mouth of babes, how can one not believe?

—**Kathy Keidel**

Angel From Cucamonga

After three decades, the jig-saw pieces of my puzzling life finally fit together. Since recently discovering I had been sexually abused as a child, I was experiencing excruciating emotional pain. My faith had been shaken to the very core. And I had withdrawn from most Christians because so many had responded to my pain by dumping salt in my wounds.

I drove to a nearby lake. As I walked by the softly lapping water, tears streamed down my face and I screamed, "Do you hear me or even care, God? I'm at the end of my rope. Suicide is the only answer!" In the midst of my pain, I found myself gathering rocks.

With the largest rocks I formed a circular base. Upon this I stacked smaller rocks, decreasing in size as they tapered to a point. It was an act of my will—I felt nothing!

Suddenly I saw so vividly what I had been studying in the book of Genesis. After being harshly mistreated by Sarah, Hagar fled into the wilderness. No doubt Hagar felt angry, confused, and hurt. So did I!

Then the angel of the Lord appeared to her. And though he didn't promise to change her circumstances, he did promise her she would have a son and many descendants. There was no question in Hagar's mind that God Himself had spoken to her. God cared about her when she was running in the opposite direction!

She named that place "Beerlahairoi." It means, "The well of the Living One who sees me." God saw . . . God heard . . . and God came to her—right where she was.

I looked at my rock altar and realized this was my "Beerlahairoi." That simple act of building an altar sparked within me the realization that I too have a God who sees and hears me . . . and who cares about my pain! I knelt facing the altar. I vowed to trust a God I wasn't sure could be trusted. I vowed to believe my God guarantees that justice will ultimately triumph over evil. But more than anything else, it was simply a vow to go on—rather than give up!

The sense of peace and hope that flooded my soul convinced me I could make it with God's help. I knew He would be there for me no matter what; no matter how I felt.

Enthusiastically I gathered more large rocks—for a different purpose. I placed them on a huge boulder jutting into the lake. From that rugged platform I ceremoniously heaved them in. Each rock represented a different element of my pain: Rejection . . . Anger . . The Denials . . . The Rebukes . . . Toxic Christians . . . Hatred . . . Bitterness . . . Confusion . . . Betrayal . . . Grief.

With each succeeding burial, marked by a satisfying splash, I felt more resolve to make it through this ordeal. God had personally met me in my hour of despair!

A few days later I took my 7-year-old son, Adam, to the lake. We found the altar intact, and I briefly explained what it represented.

An older gentleman was fishing nearby. We decided to hike around the point. On our way back to the altar Adam asked, "Mom, why don't you tell that man about Beer-whatever-it's-called?" I responded with the excuse that the man wouldn't understand. But as we rounded the point Adam loudly insisted I tell him. Through clenched teeth I pleaded with Adam to be quiet.

But it was too late. Amused, the stranger asked, "Tell me what?"

I sheepishly said, "Do you know what Beerlahairoi means?" He smiled and answered, "Yes. Do you know what Jehovah Jireh means?"

I was dumbfounded! Then I smiled and replied confidently, "Yes, it means God will provide."

He nodded.

I showed him the altar. I explained I was struggling through a painful crisis; but I had placed myself and my problems in God's hands. He shared how God had been faithful to him in life's darkest moments.

His name was Troy and he lived in Cucamonga. He asked if I was going through a divorce. Before I could stop it, the story of the sexual abuse tumbled out.

I was spilling my guts to a complete stranger, a man I did not know and yet I felt as if I did know him! He was different—he didn't offer the usual trite, pious platitudes. Just being near him I felt accepted, understood, and encouraged!

As the sun set we walked to the parking lot together. Troy extended his hand and said, "I'll really be praying for you and your family, Jo." Shaking his hand, I thanked him, and we went our separate ways.

Driving home I could hardly contain my excitement over meeting this "stranger," who we discovered was our brother in Christ. But as I pondered this unusual encounter, I finally grew silent. *Who is this man who compelled me to feel I was in the very presence of God? Is he a mere man*, I wondered.

I don't know if angels wear Levis, drive cars, or go fishing . . . but I believe it's possible!

—Jo White

Mysterious Guest

During the Great Depression, money and food were scarce. Pearl Underwood's widowed mother had to care for her older brothers and herself, yet she trusted God to care for them. Several weeks before Christmas, Pearl's mother began putting aside small amounts of flour and sugar for baking her special sweet cookies. When baking day, a Saturday, finally arrived, Pearl and her brothers awoke to find a deep snow had fallen overnight.

As the children's mother pulled pan after pan of fragrant cookies from the oven, the kids tallied up the various reindeer, stars, bells, and gingerbread men. Suddenly she exclaimed, "This one looks like an angel!" Sure enough, what were supposed to have been the arms of a gingerbread man had spread upward and out, just like angel wings.

"Please, Mother, can't we eat just one?" the kids begged.

"No," she replied, "Not until I'm finished baking. But I'm really surprised. I never got so many out of a batch before."

Finally she placed the last cookie on the table to cool, then led the children once more into the living room to thank God for their bounty. "Dear Jesus," she prayed, "You've given us so many cookies—far more than we ever expected. Won't you send some hungry person to help us eat them?"

Cookies and milk never tasted so good as they did that wintry morning. As they ate, they talked about the deep snow in their yard, and that not even one footprint marred its beauty.

Later that day they heard someone knocking on their door. When Pearl's mother opened the door, there stood the strangest little man Pearl and her family had ever seen. He was not much taller than Pearl, and his shabby, old fashioned coat made him seem almost as round as he was high. His hair, sticking out from under a battered old earmuffed hat, was a glistening, snowy-white. And never before or since, has Pearl seen such deep, heavenly blue eyes. In her memory, she can still see that man's rosy, chubby-cheeked face.

"Could you please give me something to eat?" he asked the woman who stood at the door. "I'm very hungry, and terribly cold."

"All I can give you is a couple of fried egg sandwiches and some cookies," she replied, "But you are welcome to what we have. Would you like to come in to warm up while I fix your sandwiches?"

"I'll come in to get warm," he said softly as he took off his hat and gloves, "But if you don't mind, I'll take the sandwiches with me."

When the sandwiches were ready, Pearl's mother wrapped them in waxed paper and put them in a paper bag, along with an orange and a big handful of the cookies she had just made. Of course, Pearl and her brothers had already agreed to share their extra cookies—but to give away one of their precious oranges? Like most children during the Depression, they considered an orange almost as valuable as a chunk of gold. But they knew better than to question their mother's generosity.

As their visitor left, he thanked the kind woman and added softly, "God bless all of you," then went out the door. Pearl and her brothers all ran to the windows to see which way he went, but he was nowhere in sight.

"Where did he go, Mother?" Pearl asked.

She opened the door, and the footprints he had made coming in were still there. Yet not one footprint showed that he left our house or our yard.

Ignoring the icy cold, the children bundled up and trudged over to the neighbor's house to tell about their mysterious guest. However, no one had seen him except them. They went further down the road but he had simply vanished. Half frozen, the children hurried back into the house to tell their mother about their futile search.

"Well," she answered as though she understood a deep mystery, "You can look all you want, but I don't think you'll find him. You saw the footprints he made coming into our house, but there were none to show his leaving. We'd have seen them if they'd been there, because he was the first to walk in that fresh snow."

"But where could he have gone?" the children continued to ask.

"I don't know," she replied. "But didn't we pray that God would send us someone who was hungry? He sent someone, didn't He? I believe that little man was an angel. God must have sent him to see if we really meant it when we said we were willing to share our Christmas cookies."

—Georgia Burkett

BEST INTENTIONS

ONE day, I taught my young class the story of Jesus visiting Mary and Martha. I carefully explained how Martha had hurried to clean the house and cook a special meal. Then I paused and asked, "What would you do if Jesus was going to visit your house today?" One little girl quickly responded, "I'd put the Bible on the table!"

—Louise Day

Angels In Disguise

My teenage marriage had just ended in divorce and I was alone and penniless with two babies to support. The day my landlord told me I must give him at least twenty dollars by the end of the week or move out, I fell to my knees in desperation and asked God to help me.

Without work experience of any kind, I took the first job offered to me—waitress on the night shift of a busy restaurant. On my first night on the job, a derelict—that's the only way to describe this scroungy-looking piece of humanity—came through the door and sat at my counter. His matted gray hair, his tobacco-stained teeth above a whiskery chin, and his torn and dirty clothes instantly repulsed me. But something in his voice, melted my stony heart. "Say, girlie, I'm hungry. Could you spare some soup?"

I checked the paper cup where I had been throwing my tips and found there were just enough coins to buy him a large bowl of soup, a cup of coffee and a slice of our famous homemade pie. When he finished, he thanked me, and left.

That little display of generosity caught the attention of customers, co-workers and manager. I was not only ribbed for being such a soft touch, but also warned by the manager never to do such a thing again. "After all," he declared, "We can't give free handouts to every bum on the boulevard!"

Tears sprang into my eyes. I don't know if they reflected self-pity, anger or humiliation, but as they came spilling down my flaming cheeks, I began to sputter, "Well, maybe none of you have been hungry or broke, but I have. Besides, it says in the Bible, 'Give and ye shall receive'." Now my tormentors really roared, but I finally composed myself and returned to work.

The rest of the evening passed uneventfully. Then, just before closing time, a nice-looking, well-dressed man walked in. He scrutinized each waitresses' face, then sat down at my counter.

He gave me the name of a certain waitress and asked if she was off-duty that night. After checking with the manager, I told him that the girl he was looking for no longer worked there and no one knew where she could be reached.

The man then told me this story: "One night, about a year ago, my car went over an embankment and I came into this restaurant staggering and bleeding. Everyone ignored me, assuming I'd been in a drunken brawl. But this waitress took pity on me, called my family and a tow truck. At the time I was too dazed to give her anything for her trouble, and now I've waited too long."

The man sat in dejected silence for a moment, but then his face brightened. "Here," he said. "You take this instead." With that, he thrust a folded bill into my hand and hurried out before I could even thank him. In my hand was the answer to my prayer—a twenty dollar bill!

I felt then—as I do today—that the nice-looking man and my "derelict," too, were angels in disguise sent by God to test and strengthen the wobbly faith of a young girl in need.

—**Bettymae J. Huff**

Angels Watching Over Randy

Randy had always been a special child to our family. At three years old he didn't seem to communicate as well as his older brother. Like Rusty, Randy was a very striking child with brown hair, black eyes and clear, creamy skin.

That Sunday afternoon, in late June of 1975, it seemed to be especially hot and humid. Harold, my husband, was lying down taking a well-deserved nap before night church services. I was talking on the phone when Randy walked in with his toy dog that he pulled behind him. "Mommy, Mommy, I'm going to Bo-Bo's house." Bo-Bo is my mother and Randy was forever playing make-believe so I said, "O.K., Randy. Have fun." I continued talking to my sister for about 15 minutes.

I went out in the front yard to tell the boys to come in because of the heat. When I asked Rusty about Randy, he said he hadn't seen Randy in the past 10 minutes. I felt a little uneasy but instructed Rusty to look for him. After searching everywhere, panic rose in my throat.

I ran back to our bedroom, awakened Harold, and cried out, "Randy is nowhere to be found!" Harold began searching everywhere, but to no avail. I became hysterical. We were sure Randy either had wondered off or someone had kidnapped him!

I called my mother immediately and relayed the story to her. Mother lived about five miles away and we were separated by two very busy streets. Mother replied, "I will leave immediately and check every crossroad on the way."

As Harold called the police to report Randy missing, I drove down street after street trying to find him. "Oh, Lord, please protect him. Help us find him!" I prayed over and over again.

Fifteen more minutes had passed. Randy had been gone 45 minutes. I felt like every additional minute brought us closer to disaster. Reaching home, I found Harold starting to get hysterical. "Not Randy, not my Randy!" he kept crying.

My mother came in wide-eyed. "Have you found him yet?" By that time an hour had passed.

The police had told Harold to stay put; they would look for Randy, even though a report could not be filed until he'd been missing 24 hours. "Twenty-four hours? He could be dead by then!" I thought as my heart fell.

Mother and I got back into the car, searching diligently up and down the roads of our rather large neighborhood. The whole time we were praying and trying not to be hysterical but terrible thoughts kept running through my head. Then suddenly we drove up a road. I saw a tall, slim dark-haired woman and a younger blond haired young lady walking behind a little curly-headed boy pulling a "digger dog." Could it be?! Could God have so graciously answered our anxious prayers? "Yes, it's my baby; my sweet, sweet Randy," I shouted to mother.

Mother and I jumped out of the car, leaving the motor running. I ran as fast as I could and picked him up, crying hysterically. The dark-haired woman explained, "We saw him on a busy road about a mile from here. He'd fallen into a very deep ditch with a little water in it. But after taking him out, we couldn't get him to tell us where he lived."

The other younger woman broke in, "So we were just following him to make sure he didn't get hurt. He seemed to know the direction he was going." Mother and I cried and thanked them, then ran back to the car. We had to let everyone know Randy had been found!

Crying, Harold picked Randy up and exclaimed, "Oh, thank you, dear Lord." Suddenly it dawned on me that I had failed to thank those ladies properly and give them a ride back to their home on that hot afternoon.

Only about four minutes had passed so mother and I got back into the car to search for the women. We drove back to the same area—but they were nowhere in sight. After fifteen minutes of driving around, we finally gave up. I felt terrible that I didn't get a chance to repay their kindness.

When we got back home I didn't know whether to punish

Randy or love him to death. So I decided to scold him a little and love him a lot and leave the rest until later. Curious, I asked Randy, "Who were those ladies? Were you afraid of them?"

"Oh, no," Randy replied, "They were nice. They told me they were from God. What is an angel, Mom?"

Cold chills ran down my spine. We all sat in a circle and Harold prayed a prayer of thanksgiving and praise.

—Marilyn Goss Scogin

Lost

I had just left Boston's Logan airport in my rental car and was headed for the Massachusetts Turnpike and the Marriott Hotel. As I emerged from the maze of underpasses that led to the Massachusetts Turnpike, I read the signs on top of the buildings. My mouth dropped open when I saw the Marriott Hotel sign pass by me. *Where is the off ramp I'm supposed to take?* As *night descended upon the city,* I found a gas station at the bottom of an off ramp where the lady in the cashier's booth gave me some quick answers to my questions and waved me on.

Understanding only half of what she said, I drove down the street hoping to get some bearings in the dimly-lit neighborhood. Whenever I slowed down to read a sign, cars behind me honked. I went around and around on one-way streets looking for Huntington Avenue, which would take me to the hotel. In doing so, I completely lost my sense of direction.

"Dear Lord," I prayed aloud. "I'm lost, it's very late, and I'm scared and alone in a strange city. Help me!"

I remembered the map given to me by the car rental agency. I turned down a side street to park and check the map, but the street was filled with parked cabs. The drivers were waiting for fares or taking a break. I double-parked alongside a cab to ask for directions, but the cab driver paused and scratched his head. From the corner of my eye I noticed a woman step into the street and then walk between our cars. She said something to the cab driver that I couldn't hear. Then she leaned toward my car, put her hand on the door and spoke into the open window.

"I'm heading that way. I can direct you," she said as she opened the passenger door and settled in the passenger seat. "You know, I don't usually hitch a ride with strangers."

I was stunned at her bold actions. Was she trying to make me feel comfortable? What choice did I have? With no time to think, I answered, "I don't usually pick up strangers." I swallowed hard to keep from choking with fear. I stole a quick glance at the lady and saw a dark, short-haired woman, dressed in a navy blue suit and white blouse. "That's strange," I thought, "She doesn't even have a handbag."

She didn't introduce herself and my fear paralyzed my ability for small talk. *At least she's sitting as close to the passenger door as possible.*

The heavy silence was finally broken when she told me to drive up two main blocks and make two right turns. I negotiated the car as instructed and as I made the last turn I saw the hotel entrance on my left. " There it is," I said. "What a relief!"

I felt my body relax, knowing I would be safe. With a sigh, I drove into the left turn lane and waited for the green arrow. Now I could focus on my passenger. "Why don't I let you out at the hotel entrance?" I said scanning the area for a place to park.

"I'll just get out here," she said.

In that moment I heard the door open. When I turned, she was already out of the car and closing the door. The green arrow came on and a rush of fear rose within me as I pictured the woman crossing the street into oncoming traffic. Turning to warn her, I looked up and down the street and over all of the well-lit adjacent areas. There was no one on the sidewalk, no one crossing the street, and no cars on the street. The area was completely vacant.

"Lord, where did she go?" I whispered. I was committed to make the left turn and drove into the parking structure. "Lord, I pray she made it all right." Tired and hungry, I checked into the hotel, looking forward to the comfort and security of my room.

Later that evening, while sitting up in bed, I planned for the next day. My thoughts strayed to the problem of finding the hotel. I thanked God for answering my prayers for safety and the woman's directions. With a sigh, I picked up my Bible from the nightstand for my usual evening reading. The pages fell open to Hebrews 13, and I read verse 2, "Do not forget to entertain strangers, for by so doing some people have entertained angels without knowing it."

—Irene Carloni

Leviathans Come In All Sizes

My son, David, was ten at the time. We had been sitting in the den watching a television show about unusual things people have seen and experienced. After the show we had a few moments of discussion concerning what we believed and didn't believe about ghosts and crop circles, I decided it was time to turn the lights on and start supper for the two of us. My husband wouldn't be home from work until after midnight.

David had more to say, so he followed. Through years of experience, I knew right where to find the light switch, so we navigated freely through the dark house in our stocking feet. "I should have turned on the lights earlier," I said.

Suddenly, I heard David let out a gasp. Then he yelled, "Turn on the light. I stepped on something."

Flipping on the switch, I looked down. A four-inch-long centipede was navigating its rust-colored and segmented body across the kitchen floor. Something was nagging at the back of my mind, but I had to get rid of the centipede. Grabbing the fly swatter, I finally managed to kill it.

We put it in a jar to show my husband. Still shaking, we made ourselves some sandwiches, said a heart-felt blessing, then ate the sandwiches while pulling our feet up under us as we sat on the sofa. I was trying to figure out how to ask David about something without planting ideas in his head. He spoke first.

"Mom, something pushed me."

"Pushed you? What do you mean?"

"I don't know. It was just a little push and my foot landed in a different spot. Otherwise, I would have landed on the other end of the centipede," he explained. "I saw a flash of light."

That was what I had wanted to ask him because I, too, had seen a light. It was only a flash—light so white, it was almost bluish. I had the impression that it was in the silhouette of a shrouded person. I asked him where he saw it and he said it was by the left side of his face.

That was the same area I'd seen it. Then, without describing anything, we went into different rooms and each drew what we'd seen. When we compared them, they were the same thing from two different viewpoints. He was closer so saw less, but saw it straight on. I was farther and saw it almost from head to waist and in profile. His description of the color was "white."

David said in awe, "Mom, I think it was an angel."

"So do I and it gently nudged you because angels aren't rough. It only needed to be sure you didn't land on the stinger." We both got tears in our eyes and felt very honored that God would allow us to see the angel He sent to protect David.

—Nancy E. Peterson

2

Christian Living

I urge you, therefore, brethren, by the mercies of God, to present your bodies a living and holy sacrifice, acceptable to God, which is your spiritual service of worship.

Romans 12:1

Neighbors In Disguise

Hearing the thump of a flat tire, I groaned inwardly. I was taking two young nieces home after their summer visit and this would make the trip seem longer. As I pulled off the highway, I prayed silently for help. It had been many years since I'd changed a tire, and never on this car which had a kind of jack I had never used.

Even before the trunk was unlocked, I realized the girls' determination to see everything wouldn't make it easy for me to keep them away from the highway traffic while I worked on the left side of the car.

Before I could unload the trunk to get at the jack and spare tire, I had a more urgent concern. Two huge motorcycles stopped behind us and their burly, bearded riders in leather jackets dismounted. Everything I'd ever heard about the depravity of motorcycle gangs raced through my mind as they approached us. *Don't show fear,* I told myself.

"Need help, lady?"

The disarming approach . . . "Oh, no thanks. I can do it."

"Uh, well, you really should put your blinkers on. The Highway Patrol is right fussy about that."

When I turned to attend to that, with a wary eye on the girls, the biker added a reminder to set the hand brake. I hadn't thought of that either. Embarrassed and appalled by the possible consequences of forgetting vital safety measures, I attended to them in silence.

By that time, one biker had the jack in place and the other was lifting out the spare tire. Clearly they intended to change that tire whether I admitted needing help or not. I decided to concentrate on keeping the girls away from the highway—and the bikers—while they worked.

That wheel, which hadn't been removed since we owned the car, proved very difficult to take off. Long before they succeeded in breaking it loose with sheer brawn, I knew all too clearly that

I couldn't have done it alone. Suddenly I was ashamed of my first ungracious response to their offer of help. With some embarrassment I realized my fear came from my long-standing suspicions about bikers.

When the tools and damaged tire were stowed away, I shook hands with the men, thanked them and offered to pay for their help. They waved aside the offer with boyish grins, climbed on their machines and roared away.

Samaritans in disguise, I thought. Then I remembered that the original "good Samaritan" of Christ's parable was from a group despised and mistrusted—probably even by the person he helped. Suddenly I knew this beloved parable wasn't only about caring. It was also about prejudice.

I had just received a private lesson about pre-judging others, plus a reminder that even today the Lord may surprise us with the people he sends to meet a need. Those bikers were Samaritans—neighbors in disguise.

—Florence Ferrier

Just Passing Through

Our son-in-law, Mark, is a fighter pilot. One time during a visit, he was able to let me experience what it is like to be a pilot by using the F-15E flight Simulator. I sat in a virtual cockpit with video screens all around me recording my speed, altitude, and ability to keep the plane level and on the right course.

I was a couple of minutes into the flight when Mark, who was in the back seat, calmly told me over the earphones, "Oops, you just crashed! Let's get you up and going again."

As I later reflected on this experience I thought, *How like the Christian life!* The evidence indicated that I had crashed, but since it was only a simulation flight I was still alive, able to recover and resume flying. And so it is with us. We may be struck down, but we cannot ultimately be destroyed because we have been born again to eternal life. Our lives are now hidden—concealed, safe, secure in Christ with God (See Colossians 3:3).

—Cynthia Heald

Who's In The Driver's Seat?

With a rumble of shifting gears, the 65-foot tanker eased onto Interstate 5 at Oceanside, California. Her tanks empty after dumping a load of gasoline at Camp Pendleton, Linda Kangrga headed north on the freeway to pick up her "going-home" load in Orange County on the day before Father's Day, June 19, 1993. The ocean breeze through the open window stirred her long, blonde hair under her Western-style black hat. She had turned her life over to Christ just two weeks before.

When she got her rig up to speed, the 33-year-old moved it into the number 3 lane. Then, a couple of miles later, a black Jaguar veered in front and cut her off.

Instantly her mood turned foul. Forced to downshift, she slammed on her brakes. "Idiot!" she yelled aloud. "Don't you know how dangerous that is? Two can play that game."

She swerved left into the number 2 lane (a serious offense for big rigs), roared ahead of the couple in the Jaguar, cut back in front of them and hit the brakes. The moment she stepped on her brake pedal, she remembered her newfound faith and conviction gripped her heart. Sucking in her breath, she confessed, "Lord, I'm sorry! Please forgive me! I could have endangered that couple's lives."

The Jaguar pulled out from behind and sped on, fading into traffic. Just then Linda noticed in her left side mirror two helmeted motorcyclists.

Oh, my gosh, she shuddered. *Those guys must have seen the whole thing. God, have mercy.*

Ten minutes later she reached the San Onofre Inspection Station and truck scales. On Saturdays the scales were closed, so trucks simply slowed as they drove through the empty lane and continued on their way. Linda eased her tanker into the lane, when suddenly she saw a California Highway Patrol officer step from behind a partition. He signaled her with an angry jerk of his thumb to pull into an inspection bay.

As she maneuvered into the bay, the officer got into his patrol car and drew up in front of her. At the same time another CHP cruiser parked behind her truck, trapping her.

Linda felt her blood run cold. *Lord, no! They're going to arrest me for reckless driving!*

The officer in front strode over and yanked open the driver's door of Linda's cab. "Do you want to tell me what's going on?" he demanded.

Linda tried to keep her voice steady while her heart pounded. "What do you mean, sir?"

"You were screwing around on the freeway. You want to tell me what happened back there?"

As calmly as she could, and without lying, Linda answered, "Well, I did have an encounter with a black Jag. I made a lane change but the Jag took off."

The CHP officer turned and motioned. Out from behind the partition came the two motorcyclists.

I didn't notice them passing me! Now they've got two witnesses, and they're going to make me pay for my stupid mistake—maybe cost me my job. Lord, help!

One of the pair, a lumberjack-sized man, pulled his bike over to Linda's door. He looked up at Linda, staring dumbfounded.

"Where—where's the guy?" he finally sputtered.

"Pardon me?" Linda said.

"Where's the guy who was driving this truck? What happened to him? You must have stopped and let him out back there."

"No, sir," replied Linda, puzzled. "I'm the only one driving this truck, and I don't carry riders."

The biker still shook his head in disbelief, as though to erase Linda's image from before his eyes. "No, there was a man driving this truck," he insisted. "A man with gray hair and a long, gray beard."

What? Linda's mind spun in astonishment, as a fearful awe began to creep over her. *No way! With my window down, he couldn't miss my black hat!*

The CHP officer frowned at the motorcyclist, then looked at Linda. The shroud of confusion proved too much, and he turned back to the cyclist.

"O.K., that's all we'll need, thank you."

When the two bikers drove off, the officer addressed Linda with a different tone.

"I'm sorry, ma'am," he said courteously. "There must have been some mistake. Have a nice day now."

"Thank you, sir," Linda replied meekly as he shut her door. Then, recalling the current holiday weekend, she called out her window, "Happy Father's Day."

Quivering inside and out, Linda steered her rig slowly through the bay and headed back to the interstate. No sooner had she merged into traffic from the bypass on-ramp, her hand still clutching the gearshift, than the tears began to flow. She couldn't explain what had happened, but whatever the two men saw, she felt convinced that the Lord sat in her driver's seat.

It was like He covered me, Linda marveled, so they saw Him and not me.

The more she pondered God's grace in sparing her from well-deserved punishment, the more she bawled aloud, her mascara streaking in wavy black rivulets down her cheeks.

How could I not love and serve You with my whole life? she prayed. *Please teach me to tame my temper and learn patience. I want to be like You, Lord. Today I give myself to You again.*

Linda sensed the warmth of God's love surrounding her and drying her tears. As she pulled into the refinery to fill up with her going-home load, she glanced toward the blue sky with a soft smile. "Happy Father's Day, Dad. I love You."

—Jane Rumph

The Two Bulletins

My husband had a touch of the flu so I was alone as I entered the church that Sunday morning. A woman I knew slightly had arrived in front of me, and we greeted each other as the usher handed us each a bulletin—clean, smooth, and colorful.

Because we were both alone, we sat together in a pew near the middle of the sanctuary. I used my bulletin to follow the order of worship, even though I knew it by heart, and to check the numbers of the hymns and the Scripture being used today. When the hour was over, my bulletin was still as clean and new-looking as before.

But I had noticed my pew mate scribbling on hers all through the service. Now as she started to put it into her purse, she saw me watching, and her face got a little pink.

"I couldn't get along without my bulletin this week," she said with a laugh.

I must have shown my surprise. "I always just throw mine away." What value could a bulletin be after the service was over?

"Oh, I couldn't do that!" She handed me the bulletin she was saving and explained each entry.

By the hymn listing of "Sweet Hour of Prayer" was a note. "Marie . . . Favorite . . . Cleveland . . . Pray . . . Write."

Marie was an old friend who now lived in Cleveland. She had come to mind because this had been her favorite hymn, but now there would be a prayer and a note from an old friend for her.

Near the Bible text was another notation. "Call Anne . . . Alone . . . Dinner." Anne was a recently widowed older woman from our congregation. The Bible verse had brought her to my friend's thoughts.

Another note, beside the announcement of our Women's Association meeting in this week's "Calendar of Events," said, "Call Ginny . . . Pick-up." Ginny was someone new in town.

Other events on the calendar had a star beside them—events she would be going to. A few had a "pray" notation—events she was not personally involved with.

Along one margin was "Prayer List." It had the names of those Pastor had said were in the hospital, sick at home, or having other trouble. I had said a brief collective prayer for them at the time, but could not have repeated all the names now, I was sure.

Most of the rest of the "white space" on the bulletin was filled with notes from the sermon. This woman had really listened. Some of the points she had underlined I had already forgotten.

"I go over this for my devotion tomorrow," she told me hesitantly. "Sometimes when I think again about what Pastor said, I get completely new ideas. Like when you read an old familiar Bible chapter and it suddenly comes to life in a different way."

I nodded; that had happened to me, but I never thought about a sermon being like that.

"I always mean to bring a pad to write on so my bulletin won't get all messed up every week," she confided as we walked out together. "But I always forget. I end up ruining the bulletin."

I thought of my own bulletin, as clean as though it had never been used and destined to be thrown into a wastebasket within a half hour. Hers looked terrible, but it was still serving her, others, and the Lord—and would be all week.

I patted her arm. "Don't worry. Maybe bulletins were meant to be written on, and I'm going to start writing on mine next Sunday."

—Betty Steele Everett

Prayer For A Housewife

Dear Lord Jesus,

As I go about my housework
Let me see each job I do,
As a service for my King
And a way of loving You.

Let me wash away my judgments
Of others right or wrong,
As I wash up the dishes
Place within my heart a song.

As I clean up little fingerprints
And lots of muddy shoes,
May I remember how you cleaned the feet
Of the loved ones you did choose.

As I mend up torn pajamas
And sew a button on,
Show me where I need to mend a breech
That's gone on far too long.

Let me tidy up my thoughts
As I tidy up the toys,
Let me sweep away my fears
Like the dirt from little boys.

May I be just as quick with my forgiveness
As I am with mop and broom,
Sweeping up the clutter
In my heart and living room.

May I rinse out pride and ego
As I rinse the bathtub out,
And while we are at it Lord
Let's take care of anger, hate and doubt.

Please remind me often Lord
That the way I'm called to serve,
Is an honor given me
And not below what I deserve.

You know Lord, as I look
At all the work we need to do,
I think we'd better house clean
At least each day or two.

—Melanie Hubbard

I'm getting so old that all my friends in heaven will think I didn't make it.

Faithful Over Little

We were in the old industrial area of Tucson. Finding no street parking, my husband parked in the alley. Weary from shopping, I waited in the pickup.

An elderly man came limping down the alley, pushing a grocery cart containing a shopping bag and a small bundle. Although the day was warm, he wore an old overcoat, so he was likely one of the street people who carry their few possessions wherever they go.

He stopped by a dumpster, which had a small pile of litter beside it. Methodically, the man transferred the litter into the dumpster. He completed his cleanup by using a wood shingle from his cart to lift a soiled disposable diaper. Finally he put the few aluminum cans he found into his cart.

Working along the back doors of the buildings, where I couldn't see, the man returned three times to put trash in the dumpster. After adding more cans to the cart. He limped off on what was probably a regular route.

I found this silent ritual very moving. Most likely the cash from each day's gleaning of cans was vital to his meager existence. Yet he took time to clean up after countless uncaring people. This striking lesson on faithfulness in small matters came from someone who had very little, yet made extra efforts which probably were rarely, if ever, acknowledged.

If our half-filled sack of aluminum cans had been in the pickup, I would have given it to him. Instead I claimed a special blessing on him and gave thanks for a wordless parable I would long remember.

—**Florence Ferrier**

No More Time To Waste

A funny thing happened to me on the way to my golden years. I learned about priorities!

Too many times in my youth my priorities were misplaced. I actually read boring best-sellers. I spent hours at proper functions that I hated and went shopping or lunched with the wrong people for the wrong reasons.

My house was sterile. Windowsills dusted. Throw pillows fluffed and placed precisely in the corners of the couch. Area rugs properly aligned. Crystal polished. Silver shining. Clothes folded then arranged neatly in the correct drawer. Clean towels hung in the bathrooms. My floors would have put Mrs. Cleaver's to shame. Even the junk drawer was straightened monthly.

My kitchen was color-coordinated. The bedrooms had matching sheets, spreads, drapes, and pillow shams. The children were ordered to keep their rooms neat, beds made, and clothing picked up.

And then, one day I read a remark by Helen Hayes. She said that she found as she grew older that time is too important to waste reading a bad book. If she didn't enjoy the first page she threw the book away. Since the day I read Miss Hayes' remark, I began to alter my lifestyle.

I discovered that excitement was passing me by. I missed the beauty of living and the wonders of life. The true meaning of existence had been buried beneath layers of time wasted on frivolous matters. I awoke to the fact that I was spending my life the way society expected me to, rather than living my life the way I wanted to. And now, since I have learned to prioritize, life is joyous!

I have learned it is more important to hand-raise an orphaned kitten than to clean the refrigerator. My time is better spent walking through my garden admiring the snapdragons than to make the bed. Silk flowers aren't as beautiful as a bouquet of dried weeds in the old crock on my dining room table. The hum of the air-conditioner isn't as soothing as the soft southern breeze blowing through my opened front door. Un-waxed floors, dotted with tufts of cat hair, won't wear out any faster than highly polished floors.

My rumpled home wraps me in warmth. I sit before the fire, sipping tea, reading Emerson—no longer agitated by disorder.

This evening, even though a large dollop of tomato sauce has dribbled onto the kitchen tablecloth, the sun settling below the horizon won't wait. I toss my napkin aside, and the terriers and I dash outside. The western sky is ribboned with pink streamers. In the north a clump of gray cloud is edged with gold. I know, as I watch twilight's closing act, that tomorrow's show will be new and different. I pick a plum, clean it on my shirt, pop it into my mouth, and wipe its juice from my chin. I settle down on an old stump, and while the terriers play at my feet, I wait for the moon to rise in the east. Soon the Milky Way glows a path above me. Satisfied, I turn toward the warmth of my home.

I am grateful for growing up. Maturing. For aging! I am enjoying wonders so freely offered. Wonders I had never seen before. Wonders I had cast aside. Wonders I had considered unimportant—until now.

—Lois Erisey Poole

My Mother's Love

Lord, there was a time in my youth when
The thought of church made me yawn—
If the choice had been left up to me,
I just never would have gone.

But the choice was never left to me
Mom was very insistent—
She always made sure I went to church,
Though I was quite resistant.

Through the years I've come to realize
The reason she made me go—
For now I have children of my own,
And I, too, want them to grow . . .

In the grace and knowledge of Your love,
To ask You into their hearts—
And lean on You when they need strength,
To dodge Satan's fiery darts.

Thank You, Jesus, for my dear mother,
Who brought me up in Your ways—
For though I misunderstood her then,
I praise You for her today . . .

For through years of learning about You
I am far from being bored—
Now I'm "glad when they say unto me,
Let's go to the house of the Lord."

—Denise A. DeWald

Mighty Oaks

I was in my seventh year of single parenting when depression hit. It took some soul-searching and psychological digging for me to realize, and admit, that my depression was caused by the admission that I no longer wanted the responsibility of my family. I no longer wanted to work full time and raise kids by myself. I resented the sacrifices single parenting demanded and prolonged periods of sleep deprivation were finally doing me in. Quite frankly, I was tired. When was I going to get my turn?

It was a terrible thing to admit! And the worse part about it is that I didn't have any solutions. The thought of giving my sons to someone else to raise was unthinkable!

My Christian friends said they'd pray for me but none could offer any suggestions. They probably thought that in typical "Jeri style," I'd soon snap out of this major funk I'd gotten myself into.

In the midst of my depression, I went to the mountains with our church's single adults hoping for inspiration and encouragement from other single parents. I took many long solitary walks in the fresh air and sought guidance from the Lord. I cried about my constant exhaustion. On one of my walks, I impulsively kneeled down and selected two small acorns from the side of the road. A nearby fallen log offered a comfortable seat, so I sat with my acorns, stilled myself, and waited . . .

My daughter, I know you're tired. I never intended one parent to raise children alone. I know about hectic schedules, conflicting activities, and about the sacrifices. Let me establish your priorities of what I feel is important and the direction I want you to take.

Look at what is in your hand; acorns, seeds of the mighty oak. When left alongside the road, they are prey to squirrels, raccoons, and other animals who eat them for sustenance, not to mention becoming victims of the crushing wheels of passing cars. Yet, when placed beneath the soil and nurtured by My hand, these small acorns grow into the grand oak tree, a home and haven to birds and animals in need of its sanctuary. The oak is one of my more durable and solid creations.

Consider the two acorns in your hand, representing your sons. Yes, I agree with you, the analogy is pretty apropos as they both are a little nutty at this stage in their lives. When left unattended, their spirits can be eroded by evil influences all around them which can snatch and destroy their innocence and dignity. Crushed by the world, they will not flourish. Yet, when the seed of their soul is planted in me coupled with nurturing of your Mother love, they will become mighty giants in life as I planned them to be when I first thought of their creation. This is why I've placed these two particular boys into your hands.

In light of this, what can be more important?

I rose from my now uncomfortable log and headed back toward the cabin, cradling the two acorns in my hand, thinking "He's right, what can be more important? What book, chore, or wild and crazy girl's-night-out could ever be more important than raising godly children?"

With this new revelation, my depression did not "magically" leave me. However, I now felt more focused in my life's direction and empowered to accept the Lord's single parenting challenge. Encouraged, I knew I would not be raising these "mighty oaks" alone.

—Jeri Chrysong

3

Employment

And whatever you do in word or deed, do all in the name of the Lord Jesus, giving thanks through Him to God the Father.

Colossians 3:17

The Teacher's Quilt

When I was a child, I lived in a small town near the gold fields of California. In 1949, we celebrated our Centennial. The men grew beards and my dad, who was a teller in a bank, wore a top hat and tails to work. Mother and I wore bonnets and long dresses.

As a town project, each family embroidered a square for a quilt. They tried to be creative, but the main objective was to include all the names of each family. The quilting club sewed all the squares together and finished the quilt. During the festivities, the quilt was raffled off. My best girlfriend won it and all the memories along with it. I loved to visit her—and the quilt.

When I was in the fifth grade, my teacher had each student embroider a square. She then had it made into a lap quilt. I remember seeing her when I was a young adult. I noticed that she had the quilt in her car. The memory of those two quilts stuck with me through my career as a teacher. I thought that some day I would have my students make a Teacher's Quilt.

One year I actually had each student embroider a square. For Open House, I pinned all the squares up on the bulletin board side-by-side and simulated a quilt. Everyone thought it was wonderful, but when Open House was over, I took the squares down, stuffed them a bag and never finished the project. Through the years, I added other scraps to the bag, forgot the squares, and accidentally gave it away to a church rummage sale.

Years later, Virginia Clouse, an elderly friend from the church came knocking at my classroom door. School was over for the day and I couldn't imagine why she was there. Out of a paper bag, she pulled the finished quilt made of the squares of my past students. She had found the forgotten scraps and put the quilt together especially for me. I cried with joy and she cried with pleasure in having used her talent to bless me.

The names on the quilt are those of firemen, beauticians, businessmen, teachers, and others. I took the quilt and visited my old students—as many as I could find. We all reminisced and revisited the past sewn in the squares of the Teacher's Quilt.

—Karen Robertson

ALL IS CALM

As our family was eating dinner one evening before Advent began, I asked, "Who can tell me what the four candles in the Advent wreath represent?" Luke my seven-year old, exuberantly began, "There's love, joy, peace, and . . . and . . ." Eager to keep up with her brother, six-year old Elise excitedly broke in, "I know: peace and quite!"

—Michele Hardie

A Radish Grows Integrity

"Mrs. Wilkins, Mrs. Wilkins. I just saw a girl pull a radish out of our garden and go into the girls' bathroom," Sam exclaimed as he entered our Kindergarten classroom breathless.

The children in the room suddenly got quiet. All eyes were on me.

"Who was it?"

"I don't know her name." Sam added. "She's bigger."

"She shouldn't pick our plants," Tiffany said angrily.

"Those are ours!" Jason chimed in.

"Boys and girls, I need to go and talk to the girl privately. Please stay in your seats and finish your work. Mrs. Stubbs is in the next classroom. She'll help if you need anything."

I opened Bev's door, motioned that I needed to leave for a few minutes and left my classroom door opened to hers.

As I entered the bathroom, a little girl, about six or seven, was washing radishes in the sink. I stopped in the doorway. She quickly put them behind her back. The muddy drips fell behind her onto the floor. She stood frozen, staring at me.

"I bet you enjoy watching our garden grow. What's your name?" I smiled.

"Kelli," she said seriously.

I walked closer to her and knelt down.

"Do you know who planted the garden?"

"Kindergartners," she said softly now looking down at the floor. She spotted the muddy drops and quickly stepped on them to cover her tracks.

"That's right," I continued. "Before they could plant seeds, they had to remove all the rocks in the soil. They've watered the garden and pulled the weeds. It was hard work. They're only five years old. Would you like a garden?"

"I'd like that. I wish we had one in first grade."

"I bet you do. It's fun to watch gardens grow and we've learned a lot. Just yesterday, we found a ladybug sitting on a radish leaf sunning itself.

"I like ladybugs," she added.

"I wonder, if you were a ladybug, would you like to sit in the dirt or on a soft green radish leaf in a garden floating up and down in the wind?"

"A green leaf." She looked down at the floor again.

I got close and put my arm around her.

"Will you do me a favor?"

"Uh huh."

"Please watch over our garden for us. If older kids start to pull out any of the vegetables, tell them in a nice voice that the Kindergartners worked hard to plant their garden and not to take any plants away. Will you do that for me?"

"O.K."

"I'm glad I can count on you, Kelli." Then I left.

About a week later, I spotted her looking at our tomato plants.

"Hi, Kelli. How ya doin'?" I knelt down and pulled some weeds.

"You know what, Mrs. Wilkins? My friend, Ryan, wanted to pick a carrot this morning when no one was looking." I stopped picking weeds and looked at Kelli. This was important.

"I told him it belonged to the Kindergartners," she continued, "And they worked hard to make it."

"Thanks a lot, Kelli." I gave her a hug. She smiled and happily skipped away.

A few days ago Kelli was caught stealing a radish. Today, she was caught with integrity.

—Sharon Wilkins

Patience—I Prayed For It Every Day

One school term I prayed for patience.
I wanted to be "cool, calm, and collected"
as I taught my third graders.

That was the year Michael was in my class,
the middle one of three boys.
His parents acknowledged that
the sickly older son and the baby demanded
most of their time.
So Michael had little attention at home.
But when he tipped over his chair,
came to class late,
teased the girls,
copied from other children's papers,
and fought on the playground,
he received lots of attention.
I scolded him day after day.

So I asked, "Lord, why aren't you giving me patience?
I pray for it every day."

Then there was Joe.
Daddy had left home;
mother worked all day.
Grandmother took care of him and his brothers and sisters,
as well as her own.
Joe was sneaky,
stole things from the children,
lied to everyone,
wouldn't do his work until I kept him after school.

"Lord, why aren't you giving me patience?
I pray for it every day."

There was Carl,
a pleasant boy when things went his way.
But if anyone crossed him,
when he failed (or thought he did),
when someone laughed at him (or he thought they did),
his face tensed angrily,
his eyes blazed,
his fists clenched.
And he retaliated by hitting or kicking
whoever was near him,
until I was worn out taking care of him.

"Lord, why aren't you giving me patience?
I pray for it every day."

There was Mary,
a sweet, pretty child, but so disheveled,
with her uncombed hair and wrinkled, dirty clothes.
No daddy,
mother too busy with her boyfriends
to spend time with Mary.
So, like a shadow,
she clung to me.
Whining and hanging onto my arm,
in the classroom, on the playground,
everywhere I went.
My heart ached for Mary,
but there were thirty-three other children
who also needed my time and attention.

"Lord, why aren't you giving me patience?
I pray for it every day."

Wearied by the constant problems,
I searched for ways
to give positive attention and love
to the children who sought it so desperately.
Then one day Michael sat in his chair
for an entire period without tipping over,
Joe told the truth,
Carl controlled his temper,
Mary played with a classmate,
and their faces beamed when I praised them
for their good behavior.

Slowly—ever so slowly—they began to improve.
And the more I praised them,
gave them stickers for good citizen charts,
happy face notes to take to parents,
and free time for good days,
the better they became.
Until one day I realized
the Lord had answered my prayer.
For His Word says,
". . . tribulation worketh patience;
and patience, experience;
and experience, hope" (Romans 5:3-4).

"Thank You, Lord,
for answering the prayer
I prayed day after day."

—Marjorie K. Evans

Even Unto These

While walking briskly down "C" hall, I heard a tiny, weakened voice calling out to me from the dimly-lit room to my right.

"Come in here, please," it squeaked. "Can't anybody hear me?"

I hadn't worked very long in the laundry room of the nursing home, but I had learned quickly that you oftentimes pretended not to hear the feeble cries. There were never enough hours in the day to answer every one. But the urgency in the voice compelled me to leave my hamper of dirty clothes and walk into the sparsely-furnished room filled with antiseptic odors.

Her name was Ruth, and she was very sick and skinny.

"Hi, Ruthie," I said in a cheery voice. "What can I do for you?"

"Could you get me a drink?" she pleaded, as darkened deep-set eyes searched my face.

"Why, of course I can," I assured her, pouring the water into her tiny blue plastic cup.

As I steadied her shaking hands and guided the liquid to her thin quivering lips, a Bible verse from long ago crept into my mind. "Even as you give a drink of water in My name, you do it unto Me."

She drank her fill and smiling weakly, then fell exhausted back against her pillow.

"Thank you," she murmured in a labored voice.

"It was my pleasure to help you," I answered sincerely, squeezing her frail little arm with its paper-thin skin.

Returning to the hall, I continued on my way, but could not erase the Bible verse from my mind. *Even unto these my brethren.* I had heard it a thousand times before, but it had never quite hit home as hard as it did today.

Suddenly, I stopped in my tracks, my breath catching in my throat. *Oh, my heavens. If being kind to someone is the same as being kind to our Lord, the reverse is also true. Being mean to someone is the same as being mean to Jesus.*

Goose bumps covered my body as in my mind I traveled back over my days at the nursing home. I knew I deliberately avoided hall "B" so I wouldn't have to listen to Freeda. And how I walked around the nurse's station to keep from having to tell Pearl the time. I also knew I hurried to get the bibs to the kitchen before Sarah in her slobbery, hard to understand voice, could grab my arm and demand that I put one on her, I felt ashamed.

From that point on, my attitude changed. I realized these people were God's children also, and deserved to be treated with the same respect I would show my Savior. And if, in any way, could I help them maintain their dignity, it was my duty and privilege to do so.

From that point on, I tried very hard to say "Hi!" to Freeda in the same cheery voice the fiftieth time as the first. And when Pearl asked the time ten times in five minutes, I smiled, touched her arm and told her. As for Sarah—I began to put the newest bib right on top so I could tell her, as I tied it around her neck, that it was put there especially for her.

I have since left the nursing home, but if I live to be a hundred, I will never forget the lesson I learned that day from an old lady who probably felt she had nothing left to give.

—Marcia Krugh Leaser

Jawless Sally

When I was young I longed to have my teeth straightened. When I approached my father about seeing an orthodontist, his reaction was terse. "I can't afford orthodonture *and* college for any of you!" (I was the oldest of six children). "You can either go to college or get your teeth straightened. Take your choice."

I wasn't entirely stupid, so I chose education. But as soon as I graduated from college and got my first job, I sought out an orthodontist and had braces put on my upper teeth.

I was then teaching seventh and eighth grade math and science. On the first day of school, we discovered the students and I had one thing in common—most of us had "railroad tracks" on our teeth! This made me immensely popular with the students undergoing orthodonture.

Among my eighth graders was a very quiet and shy young lady who always arrived in class just as the bell rang and left immediately when class was dismissed. Although she was an excellent student, she never spoke unless called upon—she was too self-conscious. "Sally" had been born with no chin. At least none that was visible, so she was quite strange looking. Children can be very cruel, and as a result of their teasing this little girl had become isolated and alienated from her peers.

I often thought of her when I went to the orthodontist. If just having crooked teeth could make me feel so self-conscious, how must she feel because of her disfigurement? In May I went to my orthodontist for the final visit to have the braces removed and have the retainer fitted.

When Dr. James had removed the braces I asked him about Sally. "Is there anything you could do for such a problem?"

"Unfortunately, no. I can't help her. But there is a young plastic surgeon here in Ann Arbor, Dr. Reed Dingman, who is doing research on chin implants and jaw reconstruction. I understand a patient like your student can have a complete reconstruction done for little or no charge if she and her parents are willing to let him operate on her," was his reply.

I was elated! Sally could have a chance to be made whole!

As soon as I returned home I excitedly called her number. Sally's mother answered the telephone and I breathlessly told her my exciting news. At first she responded with stony silence, then attacked me for my interference.

"I'll thank you to mind you own business," she growled. "There's nothing wrong with my daughter! She doesn't need any plastic surgery and we don't need your advice. Mind your own business!" And she hung up on me.

I stood there with the receiver in my hand, shocked by her response. But upon reflection I realized she was right. I had overstepped my bounds. Of course, as her mother, she thought Sally was fine just the way she was! I had been projecting my feelings onto Sally and her family and should have known better.

I never mentioned it again—to Sally or her family—and on July first of that year we left Ann Arbor. Years later, while we were in Philadelphia, I received a letter from the Ann Arbor area which had been forwarded.

When I opened it a color photograph of a beautiful young woman fell out.

"Who's this?" I wondered. "I don't know anyone who looks like that."

Upon reading the letter I learned it was a recent photo of my former student, Sally.

After she had hung up on me that day three years before, Sally's mother had second thoughts about the matter, and had called Dr. Dingman at the University Hospital to make inquiries about his project. Eventually Sally had had several operations to construct a new jaw bone. A bone graft had been taken from her rib and used to create her "new" face—she was beautiful!

Her mother was writing to tell me of Sally's transformation and to relate that Sally had just been elected Homecoming Queen of her high school! But, she went on to say, Sally's popularity was not based on her beauty alone. The fourteen lonely years she had spent before her surgery had made her extremely sensitive and empathic to the loneliness and suffering of others. As a result, she had reached out to every lonely student in her school and befriended them. She had dozens of friends and they had all voted for Sally for Homecoming Queen!

—Nancy L. Dorner

4

Faith & Trust

And my God shall supply all your needs according to His riches in glory in Christ Jesus.

Philippians 4:19

*Getting Out Of God's Way

Christine's shriek sliced my phone call mid-sentence. "BARBARA! Hurry! Your car's rolling down the hill!"

Throwing down the receiver, I spun and raced down the hall. Grabbing the only emergency cord I could, I begged, "Oh God, dear God, please let it be empty."

Moments ago I had been leaving Christine's office, my toddler in my arms, my oldest son by my side. When the phone rang, Christine had hurried back inside, then reappeared. The call was for me.

"Honey, will you put him in his car seat?" I had asked earlier as I turned to Joshua, who at age eleven, everyone's right hand man. Christine had asked him to come to physical therapy today to distract Jonathan from his sometimes painful workout.

"Sure, Mom," Joshua said. I put his brother into his arms. At three, Jonathan was still too wobbly to negotiate the rocky parking lot safely. Down Syndrome had delayed his physical and mental development. But for his family, his cute little face spelled courage and perseverance. We regarded his features as a badge of honor: he had to work so hard for things that came so easily to others. We had brought Jonathan to see Christine faithfully since his earliest, floppiest days, trying to smooth the road a bit for him to become all God meant him to be.

Why had my husband called that day? Neither of us remember. He only recalls my cry of dismay and the phone clattering on the floor. Then my screams.

"No! Oh, no! Oh, God, please, no!"

The car wasn't empty. Through the windshield, I could see the top of Jonathan's blonde head, framed by his car seat. He was being carried backwards down the sloping driveway toward the two lane road below. On the other side of the road was a thirty-foot drop to San Francisco Bay.

As though I were falling down it myself, I felt the agony of what would happen to my little boy in the minute ahead. If the car cleared the roadway without being struck, it would crash down the embankment and end in the Bay.

"Oh Lord, not here, not now," I pleaded. Memories from Jonathan's brief but difficult life flashed through my senses. The beeps of the monitors in Intensive Care, the tangle of cords and wires from his limp body, the tug on my stomach when the doctors prepared us for the worst. We had been through many close calls and so many people had prayed for our special boy. One by one, God had healed him of his frailties. For the past year he had been so healthy we had actually begun to relax.

Could God really choose to take him now, after all He'd seen us through?

Not if my son Joshua could help it. Horrified, I saw him behind the car, straining his ninety-five pounds against the ton of metal grinding him backwards. Running awkwardly in reverse as the car picked up speed, he was on the verge of being crushed any second.

I couldn't lose two sons! "Joshua, get away from the car!" I screamed. Christine was screaming too. Even as we pleaded with him, I understood my son's heart. Everything within him would rage against giving up the battle to save his brother. I screamed again, "Joshua, you must obey, you must let go!"

At last, he jumped away from the car.

As Joshua let go, Christine and I stopped screaming. The quiet was eerie. The moment hung poised like the last drop of water from the faucet. The car seemed to hesitate, the rear wheels to shift. Now the car was moving at an angle towards the edge of the driveway, losing momentum, grinding to a halt. Almost gracefully, it came to rest against an old and faithful-looking tree.

Bolting for the car, flinging open the door, I found Jonathan unhurt, but bewildered—he had never been in a moving car all by himself before! Catching sight of Joshua right behind me, he grinned and stretched his arms wide—his way of saying, "Life—what an adventure!"

I've been behind a rolling car before. I've tried to pit my puny weight against circumstances that were way too big for me to handle. Perhaps that's why I understood Joshua's reaction all too well.

"Mom, all I could think of was that I couldn't let him die," Joshua told me later.

"All I could think of . . ." That's me all over, willing to sacrifice everything for some good purpose. And ever over-estimating my indispensability. Even if I know I need God's help, don't I often think He needs mine as well? Don't I often act as though God can accomplish the supernatural only if I stay involved?

Maybe sometimes He is just waiting for me to get out of the way and let Him take care of things before I get myself hurt. Maybe He'd like to do something truly miraculous, something I'd always remember, something I couldn't take credit for myself. Maybe He'd like me to be more like Jonathan, just going along for the ride, a little worried perhaps, but remembering I'm in good hands and ready for the rescue.

I hadn't put my car in park; that little bit of carelessness almost cost me two sons. But God chose instead to teach me a lesson about His mercy and His might. He gave me a picture I will never forget — one son trying to avert disaster, letting go in desperation and being saved. The second powerless and utterly dependent on God's own outcome.

Because Jonathan is who he is, he might always keep that sweet simplicity. And I will ever be learning from his triumphant trust as he stretches out his arms and smiles, "Life—what an adventure!"

—Barbara Curtis

About Your Timing, Lord . . .

My doctor's words over the phone left me stunned. "Ruth, the mammogram has revealed a suspicious mass in your left breast. I want you to see a surgeon."

Standing there in the middle of my kitchen that cold November day I suddenly felt alone, forsaken. *God, did You forget? I'm the one who is just getting over a car accident. Remember? I was hit by that utility truck three weeks ago tomorrow. About Your timing, Lord . . .*

I struggled to replay the doctor's phone conversation to Mark, but the words got hung up on my emotions.

"I'm not sure I could ever face anything like that," I'd always said, when anyone had talked about breast cancer experiences to me. Two of my aunts had died of that dread disease, so such stories always hit much too close to home. Now that the storyline had come home, my mind was desperately trying to decide what to do with it.

Suddenly, it was as though I were watching a performance on a screen, except I was in the picture. I saw myself responding to Mark's strong arms of comfort, steadying my voice, wiping my eyes, taking a deep breath.

"God will give us courage to face whatever we have to face," I said. "Right now it's time to take the children to school. Please don't worry. I'll be all right. I'll call the surgeon this morning."

I could tell he didn't want to leave, but his classes were waiting. I waved him out the door.

Two weeks later I lay in my hospital bed watching the flurry of activity around me. Another hour and the surgeon would begin his exploration, removing the mass and carefully searching for life-or-death cells.

"Just a little something to help you relax." The nurse took the syringe from the tray she carried. The needle did its work.

Fifteen minutes later she returned. "Ruth, are you asleep already? That shot worked fast on you. Probably because you've been so relaxed all along." She gently lifted my arm and took my pulse. I knew she was talking about resources I didn't have on my own.

Later, after the test results came back marked benign, I thought back to that cold November day when the doctor first called and to the morning of surgery when the countdown was at one hour. I recalled how miraculously and silently God's peace changed from something I talked about to something I knew for a fact. Sometimes there is no other way to learn.

—Ruth Senter

Walking Blind

I was walking with my four-year-old daughter, Allison, when she took my hand and said, *Let's pretend I'm blind. Lead me.* As I had many times in the past, I took her arm and carefully guided her through several obstacles. I saw her squinting her eyes as she peeked. Several times, I said, "Allison, keep your eyes closed. Trust me. I'm your mother and I won't let anything happen to you." Allison would close her eyes tightly—momentarily; then she would sneak a peek, just to ensure I had her best interests at heart.

It struck me that this is how I am often with my Lord. I ask Him for help, or I commit something to Him, then I take back the control, forgetting that He has said, *Trust me. I'm your Father and I will take care of you.*

—Gail Ronveaux

Dancing Boots

It was our last day at the orphanage in Mexico. I had remained hidden for hours in the kitchen, scrubbing the inside of the oven, trying in vain to remove the hardened crust from years of neglect. Finally, after calling it done and stepping into the sunlight, I discovered that the rest of my missions team had left for the beach without me. No laughter, no children . . . only the barking of dogs could be heard on a nearby hillside.

I savored the moment, breathing in the fresh scent of the sea blowing across the hills. Then I walked through the dormitory while praying for each child who would sleep in the brightly-quilted beds that night. Looking through a window over one of the beds, I was surprised to see a young boy sitting alone in the sand of the play yard. I wondered how he could have been overlooked by the beach crew.

I hurried outside but halted just inches from the lone boy. His little balled up fists were rubbing his eyes with a controlled fierceness. He just kept rubbing, up and down, up and down.

I fell to the sand beside him and held him in my arms. Still the little fists kept on churning. No sobs escaped his throat . . . not even a tremble in his rigid shoulders, just that incessant rubbing. I prayed for God to show me what to do and attempted to soothe the boy with the few Spanish words I knew, but the little fists never let up in their vigil. My own tears dropped to the ground between us.

The laundry woman passed us on her way to the clothesline. I was so excited to see another adult, I jumped up and frightened her in my enthusiasm. "Por favor," I said. "A little boy needs help."

She dropped her laundry basket on a concrete slab and marched over to address the boy in his native tongue. He answered concisely, but still those little brown fists continued to rub. "His name is Antonio," said the worker. "This is his first day here." Then, without another word, she returned to gathering the row of faded shirts off the line.

First day? And no one here to greet him . . . no substitute parent, no other children . . . just me?

I plopped on the ground next to Antonio and sobbed, feeling an overwhelming sense of inadequacy. After a few moments of unrestrained weeping, I felt little hands reaching around my neck and giving a squeeze. I looked down to see Antonio's dark eyes probing mine. I pulled him close and wished with all my heart I had something more to give him.

We were still clinging to one another when laughter rolled through the air and fifty pairs of feet ran across the sand of the playground. Antonio looked out at his new world with frightened eyes. Suddenly, a shadow fell over him as Brett, the youth pastor, stood over us. "Hey, young man," he said. "I have a pair of boots here that don't seem to fit anybody. But these boys think you are the right size." Three heads bobbed their approval while Antonio's eyes grew wide with surprise.

Brett reached down to unbuckle Antonio's sandal. Every boy there held his breath while first a sock was slipped over Antonio's foot and then the boot. A perfect fit! Antonio screamed with delight and jumped up to run across the yard. He twirled in circles and raced back and forth, seeing how fast the new boots would run. He danced around his three new friends and jumped over rocks. Then, one of the older boys slipped an arm across Antonio's shoulders and walked with him as though they were a couple of buddies.

My gaze followed the two boys until they were standing on the porch of the dorm. Just before they entered the door, Antonio reached up to whisper into his new buddy's ear. Then, he turned and ran towards me, his face alight with wonder and newfound joy. He grabbed me in a hug that nearly toppled both of us to the sand, threw a bunch of Spanish words at me and ran off to catch his new friends.

I'll never forget those dancing boots. How was it that Brett had saved one pair of boots that just happened to fit the feet of a little boy he had never met?

There are times when I feel inadequate to reach out to the enormous need around me. Then, I remember the dancing boots and how God filled my empty arms with a rigid little boy and heard the groanings of both our hearts. I am encouraged to continue in the small things God has set before me—to give a smile to the busy clerk in the grocery store, to take a few of my freshly baked cookies to the lonely neighbor across the street, to take the time to read my grandchild a favorite story, to look into the eyes of someone bound to a wheelchair—bringing joy to a world that is crying for love.

—Sandy Cathcart

Jumping Jehosaphat

Some friends were getting ready to move and needed a home for their dog, Fredda. We already had a dog (Fredda's mama) but felt obligated to take Fredda back since we had given her to them "fraudulently." I thought she was a he when I gave Fredda to them, and they therefore named her Fred. After arriving home with their little guy, they noticed Fred had problems that would require surgery or a change of name. They kindly opted for a name change.

Fredda was a kind-of-cockapoo. Actually, she thought she was a kangaroo (no doubt the result of her early identity crisis) and developed a unique straight-up-and-down leap. She was a very sanguine dog and hated to be left outside. So she used her incredibly high leap to peek in our windows at what was going on. It wasn't unusual to be sitting at the table eating and, out of my peripheral view, glimpse a set of eager eyes and fluffy, flying ears. By the time I could turn to look, Fredda would have dropped out of sight. She repeated this Olympic feat frequently.

This caused many visitors concern about their sanity. We tended not to mention our "kangaroo" to guests until their eyes looked dazed. You could see them trying to process whether their minds were leaving them or we had been invaded by seeing-eye fur balls. With quick jerks, our friends would whip their heads to the side in an attempt to catch our mystifying mutt. Eventually we would confirm their UFO sightings to ease their troubled minds.

Fredda became our eight-year old son Jason's dog. Fredda would escort Jason to the bus stop. Jason would have to leave early because it takes longer when you're with an animal that insists on leaping up instead of forward. One morning, Jason came bursting back into the house crying, "Mom, Mom, come quick! Fredda's been hit by a car!"

I grabbed my housecoat, and as I secured it Jason added, "I think she's going to be all right, because I saw her tail wag!"

Halfway up our driveway, a lady I had never met came running toward me and right into my arms. She was crying, “I hit your dog! I’m sorry, I’m sorry.” I held her for a moment and assured her we knew it was an accident.

She sobbed, “Yesterday my cat died, and today I’ve hit your dog!”

“I’m sorry this has been such a painful week for you, and I know you didn’t mean to hit her,” I responded. I hugged her one last time and encouraged her to go on to work.

I thought how disconcerting as well as disastrous it must have been for that lady to have a flying dog, all eyes and ears, leap out of nowhere.

By the time I reached the road, my husband Les, had arrived and was gently placing Fredda in his pickup. He looked at me and shook his head to let me know she was dead. I turned to look for Jason and saw that he was back in line for his school bus. He had his eyes squished tightly shut, and his little arms were pressed firmly against his body in his attempt to not see or know the fate of his beloved, bouncing buddy.

“Jason,” I said softly.

He didn’t move.

“Jason, honey, your doggie is dead.”

He fell into my arms, allowing the swell of tears out of his flooded eyes. Then his tense little body let down and began to shake. I took him by the hand, and we walked down the hill to our house to grieve.

Many times I, like Jason, have wanted to close my eyes and not look at reality. Reality is often harsh, filled with unfairness, pain, and loss. But when I refuse to face truth, I find myself rigid with anxiety and unable to deal with life. Acknowledging and letting go of what I can’t change is the beginning of the grieving process.

—Patsy Clairmont

Through A Child's Eyes

A warm spring breeze filtered through the kitchen as I hurried to cook dinner. My husband had taken my three-year-old daughter for a walk and I was taking advantage of the reprieve. Suddenly the screen door slammed. I looked up to see my breathless daughter running toward me. Her pink cheeks accented her bright blue eyes.

"Mommy, Mommy, guess what!" she exclaimed.

"What is it?" I asked, curious as to what had cut her excursion short and caused such excitement.

"Daddy found a dead animal on the road. He picked it up by the tail and threw it up to heaven, but Jesus missed it!"

I could see the picture in my mind. There is a swamp across the road from our house. During the night one of it's inhabitants was struck by a passing car. Not wanting it to rot on the road my husband had thrown it over into the swamp.

My daughter must have expected to see two strong arms extending from the sky to catch the animal. When the animal descended back to earth, my daughter was both amazed and perplexed. Her conclusion? It wasn't that Jesus wasn't there or didn't care, He simply missed.

Oh, the beautiful faith of a child!

—Penny Shoup

My Daughter . . . Out On The Streets

"Sandy, you have to let her go."

The calmness of my husband's voice belied the severity of his words. How could I possibly allow my seventeen-year-old daughter to walk out of our lives? She had no idea of the pitfalls awaiting her. Would she sleep under some bridge? How would she buy food? What if some maniac raped her?

No. I can't just let her walk out. My heart screamed the words, but my lips remained silent. Somehow, I knew my husband had spoken God's will, but my heart couldn't accept it. I watched in despair as my daughter stuffed everything she owned into big plastic bags and dropped them out of her bedroom window.

"Michelle," I pleaded, "Wait till tomorrow. Give yourself time to think about it. You might feel differently later."

"No, I won't. I want to go and you can't do or say anything to stop me!" She threw the last bag out the window and stomped out the door.

Not five minutes later, my husband kissed me good-bye and left for his graveyard shift at work. I laid my head against the closing door as silent sobs shook my body. I don't know how long I stood there, but I had never felt as hurt, weak, and lost. I couldn't even pray.

I stumbled to bed fully-clothed and slept fitfully, terrifying dreams sweeping through my mind. My daughter . . . out on the streets alone.

I awoke with a start at the first hint of morning. *I haven't even prayed. What kind of mother am I?* "Lord, please forgive me, I just don't know what to say."

"It's okay, Sandy," I heard with my heart. "An outcry is going up for your daughter." The promise warmed my spirit, but my mind understood so little. What outcry?

The next few days were like a walking nightmare. I couldn't focus on anything except the nagging questions, "Where is my daughter? Why did she leave? Where did we fail her?" In the middle of the night, I awakened with the stomach-churning accusation, "It's 3:00 a.m. Do you know where your child is?"

Will this nightmare never end? Maybe if I had more faith or prayed more often, she would still be safe in our home.

The following Wednesday, my friend Judy approached me in the foyer of our church. "Sandy," her hazel eyes searched mine. "How is Michelle? I've been thinking about her often these past few days, especially a week ago Thursday night. I awoke with the strangest urge to pray for her."

My jaw dropped open. How could she have possibly known to pray for my daughter? I hadn't spoken of my concern for her in months. "I don't know how she's doing," I stammered. "She left home Thursday night and I haven't heard a word from her."

Thursday night! The very night Judy had been impressed to pray for my daughter.

I heard it said once that even a sigh directed towards God is a prayer. Was it possible that God had heard the very groaning of my heart?

As Judy took both my hands to pray, I felt she could see into the very depths of my soul. The guilt. The pain. All laid bare and open for anyone to see. Yet, as her tears dropped to the floor, mingling with mine, I began to feel the peace of the Lord weave its way through the confusion in my mind. Then at last I understood. In our weakness God calls on others to pray us through the storm. That was the outcry He'd promised!

Another friend sneaked up behind me. "I feel kind of silly telling you this," Robyn whispered, "But I spoke to your daughter a few days ago. I felt impressed to let you know that she loves you very much."

I returned Robyn's warm hug and quietly asked the Lord to forgive me for ever doubting His immense love. I also thanked Him for friends. I had felt alone, like no one really cared. Yet, Judy's prayers and Robyn's word of encouragement were proof that someone cared for me and my daughter. I'm sure there were others praying as well. That made it easier to face the uncertain days ahead.

My letting go was merely releasing her into the capable hands of a Loving God who promised to never leave or forsake her. He would be present in her hour of need even as He had been for me.

My daughter . . . out on the streets . . . but surely, not alone.

—Sandy Cathcart

When Our Father Knows Best

My heart sank as I watched my cat, speckled gray with age, fall into the makeshift box in my bathroom. *She can't even walk straight.* I fought the tears that stung the back of my eyelids. *Father,* I silently prayed, *I can't put her to sleep. Please help me.* I crouched down until I was eye-level with Nicky and cupped her chin in my hand. "I love you," I whispered as I gazed into her yellow-moon eyes.

Looking into her eyes, the anguish of the past three weeks came rushing back. "Rat poison?" I asked in disbelief. I stood at the cold, gray table, the smell of other animals still fresh in the room. I ran my fingers through Nicky's emaciated fur. After more than two weeks at the vet's on IVs and being hand-fed, she was still shaky. She barely ate her food. She was so weak she had trouble standing.

I picked her up and held her close. I rubbed the top of her head and along her cheeks, which in happier times, would have started her purring. But now she just looked up at me, pain radiating from her eyes.

Years ago, those huge yellow eyes set in the scrawny kitten's face would have been comical had she not been half-starved when I got her. She was so weak she couldn't even meow. It took months before we heard a semblance of voice. When at last she began to meow she must have been proud of herself. Every time I couldn't find her I'd start calling and she kept answering until I found her hiding place, usually in my closet.

Nicky loved being close to me. "The closer the better" was her motto. When I had a particularly bad flare-up of arthritis, I spent weeks at a physical therapist trying to get the kinks out. I ended up at home with a long list of exercises.

One day as I lay on my back doing knee rolls from side to side, I felt Nicky nudge my arm. As I rolled my knees the opposite direction, Nicky would jump over me and nudge the other arm.

Then I rolled over on my stomach for the dreaded leg lifts. Nicky crawled onto my backside and literally "dug" in for the duration. As I struggled to lift my leg, she would shift to one side. When she lost her balance and fell off her convenient perch, I laughed till my sides ached.

The week my mother passed away, Nicky seemed concerned. She paced the floor as I mourned my mother. Several times she tried to crawl up in my lap. At first, I resisted her. Then I realized she was only trying to comfort me in the only way she knew how. Nicky soon made herself comfortable in the middle of my skirt and just before she put down her head for her afternoon nap, she patted my hand with her paw. It was almost as though she were saying, "Don't worry, you still have me."

The tears I'd been fighting suddenly burst through. *Nicky has loved, comforted and made me laugh all these years. It's my turn to comfort her.*

I eased her out of her box, her legs limp as a dust rag. Gently cradling her in my lap, I murmured, "I love you, Nicky. God loves you, too." Once I realized God loved her as much as I did, I began to turn loose of my protective hold. Surely, the Creator of the universe who created all things would take good care of my cat.

"Lord," I whispered, "Nicky is Yours . . . " God's immeasurable comfort cradled my hurting heart. "You're as mindful of Nicky as You are of a sparrow." For "Not one of these (sparrows) will fall to the ground apart from the will of your Father" (Matthew 10:29).

No matter what happens, I know I can put my full trust in the Creator who knows what's best for all His creatures.

—**Nanette Thorsen-Snipes**

Lost Contact

I started up the rock as fast as I could, determined to "set my face like a flint" toward the peak. After a time, I came to a difficult ledge, and my breathless scrambling came to an abrupt halt. Suddenly, the rope was pulled too taut and hit me square in the eye. "Oh NO!" I thought wildly, "My contact lens is gone!" From my precarious perch I looked everywhere on the rope and sharp granite rock for a tiny, transparent lens, which could easily be mistaken for a water droplet.

"Lord Jesus, help me find it!" I prayed and pleaded, knowing the hopelessness of my search with such limited mobility. I looked as long as I could maintain my hold, praying with a sinking heart. Finally I resumed my climb with one last glimmer of hope—maybe the contact was still in my eye, crumpled in the corner or up under my eyelid. When I reached the top, I had a friend check to see if she could find it in my eye. It wasn't there. Every hope was gone.

I was disappointed and anxious about getting a new contact so far away from home. As we sat and rested, surveying the world from such a gloriously high perspective, the fragment of a verse popped into my head: "The eyes of God go to and fro through the whole earth."

God knows *exactly where my contact is* this moment from His high vantage point, the amazing thought struck me. But *I'll* never see it again, I concluded. So, still glum, I headed down the path to the bottom where the others were preparing to climb.

About half an hour later another girl set out where I had also begun my climb. She had no inkling of the missing contact. But there, at the steep bottom of the rock face, she let out an excited cry: "Hey you guys, did anyone lose a contact?"

I rushed over as she continued yelling, "There's an *ant* carrying a contact down the mountain!"

Sure enough. Special delivery! I bent down, retrieved my contact from the hardworking ant, doused it with water and put it back in my eye, rejoicing. I was in awe, as if my Father had just given me, though so undeserving, a big hug and said, "My precious daughter, I care about *every* detail of your life."

I wrote to tell my family. My dad drew a cartoon portraying an ant, lugging a big contact five times its size. The ant was saying to God, "Lord, I don't understand why You want me to drag this thing down! What use is it anyway? I don't even know what it is, and I certainly can't eat it and it's so *big* and *heavy*. Oh well, if you say so, Lord, I'll try, but it seems like a useless piece of junk to me!"

I marvel at God's ways and how He chooses to reveal His mercy in ways *far beyond* our human comprehension.

—Brenda Foltz

Short On Materials

One evening, our son, daughter-in-law, and five-year-old grandson were watching a basketball game on TV. Jordan noticed that some of the players were extremely tall. "Mommy," he asked, "Why are some people so tall and other people short?"

As our daughter-in-law pondered how to best answer his question, Jordan drew from his Sunday school knowledge and came up with his own answer. "Oh, Mommy! Is it because God didn't have enough dust to finish the short people?"

—Marjorie K. Evans

MADE TO ORDER

AT a recent church dinner, I took my three young children through the food line. As I juggled everyone's plate and drink, I told the kids to be on their best behavior. When finally seated, I sighed with relief and told them they were doing great—that we hadn't had any catastrophes yet. At that, my three-year old, Dawn, looked around and said, "Where are they, Mommy? I'll go get them."

—Valerie Kulhavy

5

Family

Do nothing from selfishness or empty conceit, but with humility of mind let each of you regard one another as more important than himself; do not merely look out for your own personal interests, but also for the interests of others.

Philippians 2:3-4

Long-Distance Celebration

The tradition of spending Christmas with my mother and grandmother continued the year after I married. By the following year, my husband wanted to spend the holiday with his family. While I fully concurred with the idea of fair play, the realization that my mother and grandmother would suffer from the Christmas blues disturbed me. Somehow I had to do more than send presents and make a long-distance call.

Words from the song, "The Twelve Days of Christmas," began to inspire me. Gifts opened on consecutive days would enhance the joy of the season, but I could still perceive the feeling of loneliness my loved ones would experience on Christmas Eve—the time when we normally exchanged gifts. I needed to build anticipation that would lead up to a momentous occasion.

A plan formed in my mind. Indeed I would send each of them twelve presents designated for the twelve days preceding Christmas. Instead of opening the gifts each day, though, they would open an attached envelope, read a clue, and try to guess the content of the package. For example, the clue that matched my mother's favorite deodorant read, "This will keep you as fresh as a Daisy." That was a play on words, because Daisy was my mother's name. I instructed them to write down the guesses to compare with the actual gifts they would open on Christmas Eve.

Money was ideal as the major gift for both women. The clue to the money tree I made for my mother read, "You always told me this didn't grow on trees, but maybe you were wrong."

Since a reward adds excitement to any game, I placed an ample supply of coins in a box labeled Bank. Each correct guess earned fifty cents. Unearned money would be donated to their favorite cause of missions.

To add nostalgia to the celebration, I composed a letter for them to read on Christmas Eve. I opened my heart and simply allowed my emotions to spill onto the paper. Then I continued with the "I remember when . . ." approach my mother had introduced to me while I was growing up.

For me, Christmas memories began when I was nearly four years old. The set of blue metal dishes I received that year made a lasting impression on me—perhaps because I liked to throw tea parties for my dolls.

While our family lived in the country, we trekked to the woods each year to cut down a Christmas tree. With strings of popcorn and a few homemade decorations added to our collection of ornaments, we trimmed the tree that provided me with hours of enjoyment.

About the time my childish wonder over presents and decorations declined, I discovered the real meaning of Christmas. Following my mother's example, I accepted Jesus as my Savior. Our shared faith had enhanced the celebration of Christmas in the past and could give us a sense of togetherness even on a long-distance basis.

As I finished my letter, I realized I had already experienced a sense of togetherness. I prayed that, although I was absent, I could project part of myself across the miles to the ones I loved. "Why don't you share some of your good memories with each other?" I challenged my mother and grandmother.

When I made my long-distance call on Christmas Day, my usually reserved mother bubbled over with enthusiasm. "It just seemed like you were here," she said.

As it turned out, that was our last Christmas celebration free from the shadow of sorrow. My mother's health began to fail soon afterward. A few years later my mother and grandmother died the same year. That is why I treasure the memory of the year I shared Christmas with my mother and grandmother although we were far apart.

In one way, though, I can still celebrate Christmas with my family through faith. In coming to bring us salvation, Jesus bridged the distance between earth and heaven, where we shall be together again. That is cause for great celebration!

—**Esther M. Bailey**

On His Shoulders

My dad was very busy when I was a child, but I could always manage to get his attention. I can still see him sitting at his desk during my preschool years. He was in the final year of his doctoral studies at the University of Southern California, and the pressures were intense. Nevertheless, my brother and I took priority. I would climb on the chair behind him and spend an hour or two on his lap or even on his shoulders. He never seemed to mind. Every now and then he would stop to toss me in the air or play a game. These moments, even more than gifts and surprises, were the way he expressed genuine love to this wide-eyed child.

—Danae Dobson

Holidays: Too Much Trouble?

I groaned as I reviewed my list. Pick up milk and donuts for breakfast, bake pies, prepare stuffing, put fresh sheets on the beds, leave time for a shower . . . *Oh, dear! Have I forgotten anything?*

"I'm already tired, and the day's only half over," I whined to my husband, Seth. "Holidays are so much work. By the time they begin, I'm too tired to really enjoy them."

I thought, *Holidays! Traditions! So much trouble! But tomorrow was Thanksgiving and our kids and their kids were on their way. I had to stop worrying and get busy. I stopped and prayed for strength to finish my work.*

As our families arrived from New York, Ohio, California, and Michigan, my spirits lifted. It was so good to see them; so wonderful to be all together! But as the noise level grew, so did my headache.

Holiday preparations were complete, and everyone was nestled into bed by 1:00 AM. I set the alarm for 5:00 so we could stuff the turkey and start it roasting. That left just four hours to sleep. "Bummer!" as the kids say.

By the time the meat, stuffing, potatoes, gravy, salads, yams, cranberries, rolls, and pies graced the table, my eyes were heavy and my feet hurt. "Remind me to give this thankless job to someone else next year," I growled softly to Seth. "I don't know if these kids even appreciate Thanksgiving."

After everyone was overstuffed, our son Dick took charge of devotions. After all, thanking God was the purpose of today, wasn't it? Though I had lost my enthusiasm, Dick approached it with energy. He carried in a huge board covered with newsprint. At the top he wrote giant words in red felt marker, I THANK GOD FOR All 19 of us, ages 2 to 57, crowded into the living room, some sitting on the floor, some in laps. I eyed the three teens. *They'll never go for this.*

Dick announced that each person could list one item for which he or she were thankful. "Who is first?" he smiled.

The smallest ones began eagerly with scrawls, drawings and misspelled words. They were so proud to put their ideas up on the board by themselves.

Then came a surprise: my teen grandson sprinted up to add to the collection! Would he be mocking, or flippant? Not looking around, he wrote quickly, "Family and girlfriend."

I sat speechless, watching every person give thanks: "Artistic talent, family relationships, warm homes, independence, another season, health, filling all life's needs, Sue's pies, salvation, Mom and Dad"—the list was filling the poster. Someone circled the big, black letters: "JESUS."

By now tears of joy blurred my vision. But I could see well enough to add my own thankful message: "A new song!" For the melody now ringing in my soul was this: "Yes! Family traditions are worth whatever it takes to make them happen again and again."

—Mary Cotton

Chiclets, Kool-Aid, And Bible Stories

I was tired. Besides, there was a good show on TV. Yet, I had not read Bible stories to my four-year-old daughter, Carey—something we did most evenings. Then, I remembered Grandma.

Grandma was 78 when I was born. I remember her as a stately woman who wore her wispy black hair pulled back into a bun. She wore a hearing aid in her left ear that connected by way of a wire to a small box she wore in the bosom of her dress. She always wore dresses—and black, sturdy shoes that laced up.

Though Grandma dressed according to the standards for older ladies of her day, she also enjoyed some of the modern conveniences, one of which was Kool-Aid. Only, instead of mixing it in a two-quart pitcher, Grandma made it one glass at a time. She would sprinkle a little of the powder into a glass, add sugar and water, and mix it up. Perhaps she was being thrifty, as she was in most areas of life.

Grandma also liked Chiclet gum. She kept a box in her dresser drawer in the den. I liked Chiclets too. I liked to pop a whole handful of the small squares into my mouth. Grandma only chewed one piece at a time. Sometimes she even cut a piece in half. I wasn't sure if she did this because she wore dentures, or if she was just being thrifty.

Grandma was also thrifty with her time, but she gave some of it to me. Before I was old enough to go to school, she would frequently place me on her lap and read to me from my big, black Bible story book. She would read and read, often until her voice grew so hoarse that she'd have to stop for awhile. From that time with Grandma, I learned many Bible stories, and began to learn about a loving God and Savior.

Throughout the years, I have remembered Grandma and those Bible stories. Now, as I looked at my daughter, there echoed in my mind a voice grown hoarse from reading. Suddenly,

I didn't feel as tired. The TV didn't seem so enticing. I took my daughter on my lap and opened the Bible story book.

Grandma died when I was twelve. Carey never knew her. Yet, as I held my daughter and read the Bible stories, I felt that Grandma was reaching across the years and touching Carey's life.

In a sense Grandma fulfilled what the Psalmist said, "They will proclaim his righteousness to a people yet unborn . . ." (Psalm 22:31 NIV).

—Cora Lee Pless

How To Be A Fun Grandparent

A classic example from one grandmother who, by her own description, is little, somewhat old, and somewhat fat:

"I just plain hated rock music. Loud, awful, terrible lyrics. I kid you not, I just plain hated it.

"Then one day I realized my three teenage grandchildren were drawing away from me. What could I do? One thing I could do was change my tune. I could take another look at their music.

"So that's what I did. I went to the library and checked out some books on rock music. Then I went to the music store, got in one of those little cubicles they have there, and really listened to some of this stuff.

"You may not believe it, but I began to get interested. I even bought some books on the history of rock music, and now I even learned some things my grandchildren didn't know. I also kept a little notebook on what I was learning, and then I'd let certain items drop to get their attention.

"Next thing I knew they were bringing friends over to talk rock with Grandma. We'd sit in the den, eat popcorn, and I'd tell them things I'd learned that they didn't know.

"Came the great day. The junior-high principal called and asked me to speak to 500 kids at his school about rock music. Five hundred kids listening to this fat little grandma talk about their music. How'd it go over? If I do say so myself, it went over like gangbusters.

"And now hang on. Very shortly thereafter the high-school principal called and asked if I would talk to the high school.

"Can you imagine me, the grandma who once hated rock music, there in this huge high school auditorium, and those kids giving me a standing ovation? And what kind of climate do you think all these shenanigans created between me and my own grandchildren?"

—Martha Shedd

Warm Dentures, Warm Heart

Art class would be more fun, but my aged father-in-law would be anticipating my visit. I made a U-turn and headed to Fountain Haven Nursing Center.

Walking swiftly into Dad's room, I said, "Hi, Dad. I brought you some bananas. How are you doing?"

"Humph!"

"That bad, huh? What's the problem, the food again?"

"Nope. It's these teeth." Then, showing me, he said, "See? They clatter."

"Try your denture cream," I replied. "Maybe it will help."

"It won't do no good," he answered, shaking his head and turning toward the wall.

"Have you cleaned them recently?"

"Nope." With that, he removed his dentures and placed them in the palm of my hand. "Here, you can do it for me."

It was not a pleasant feeling to hold his wet, warm false teeth in my hands. But at that moment the vision of Jesus, kneeling down and washing the dusty feet of his disciples, came to mind. Immediately I reached for the toothbrush and baking soda and began to scrub. A faint smile appeared on Dad's face the moment that he put the cleaned dentures back into his mouth.

"Well, Dad, aside from those clattering teeth . . ." I moved closer and patted his arm, "How are you really feeling today?"

Never long on words or expression, Dad replied, "I'm still here, ain't I?"

His watery blue eyes scanned the entire room. Then he glanced down at his unbuttoned shirt. I tried to help with the buttons, but he pushed me away, muttering, "Let me do it myself." I yielded.

Ultimately our sparse conversation lapsed into silence. We sat motionless. Then I experienced an unusual moment. Dad reached for my hand and tightened his frail, wrinkled fingers around mine. He began to whisper a prayer: "Jesus, thank You for sending Mary here today. We had a good visit. And thank You for taking good care of me for so long. I look forward to seeing You soon. Amen."

Happy that Dad had included me in his prayer, I added my "Amen" to his. When I got up from my chair, preparing to leave the room, Dad said in a barely audible voice, "Mary . . . I may not see you again."

Reality struck me and I moved back and stood beside his worn, leather chair. He looked small, childlike, yet serene. I felt like picking him up and taking him home with me.

"Sure, you'll see me again! Maybe not in this room, but we will meet again. Dad, do you know where you are going?"

His eyes met mine. "Yes, That's the one thing I know for sure." More forcefully he added, "I'm going to heaven, where I will be with Jesus forever."

After I left him, I pushed my way through the heavy exit doors. A glorious view greeted me-a view that no artist could ever splash onto a canvas. I thought that maybe this day would mark my final visit with my father-in-law here on earth, and tears welled up in my eyes. I breathed a prayer of thanks to God for the chance to be with Dad, and I headed home.

—**Mary K. Kasting**

Heritage Drives

It happened on the back road into town, while I headed for the grocery. I had driven that same route dozens of times, but this time was different. Something caught my eye. It was an old run-down, one room school house. Jagged edges of glass were all that remained in the window framing. The bell tower stood silent and empty. The weathered worn wood was bare except for a few flecks of white paint. The porch had fallen in and cows grazed on tall weeds that surrounded the building.

My foot eased off the accelerator and something drew me to the schoolhouse. As I looked through the windows, my mind brought that old building back to life. Laughter filled the air as pigtailed girls with petticoats and pinafores played with their homemade dolls or chased pesky boys around the school yard. The crack of a hand-carved bat rang out as boys in patched coveralls and worn-out shoes ran around the bases. Then a tall, elegant teacher, her hair pulled back in a bun, stepped onto the porch and rang the school bell, ending recess.

Hurried footsteps clanked on the wooden porch, into the room and to their desks. Around the corner ran a skinny boy with dark curly hair and bright blue eyes. A piece of string tied around his waist served as a belt. His arms were filled with a stack of dry wood for the potbellied stove that warmed the crisp fall air.

I knew exactly what he looked like. It was my dad. That dilapidated old schoolhouse, 3,000 miles away from my hometown, took me on a mind journey to my Dad and Sunday afternoon drives.

There were four kids, mom, dad, a dog and needless to say a station wagon. On Sunday afternoons Dad would pile four grumbling, reluctant kids in the wagon and go for a "drive." None of us were thrilled about the journey, but we knew that at the end we would pull into the ice cream shop. So the hour or so spent driving had a pretty good pay off (Besides that we had plenty of time to decide which flavor we wanted, vanilla or chocolate).

As the years have gone by, I now realize it had a longer lasting pay off than ice cream. I have heritage. Little did I know that as we peered out the windows of that station wagon, we were actually looking into the windows of our past. We drove everywhere. We went to the one room school house to which he walked a mile to school (he really did) an hour early to stoke the fire; and to the river hole where he spent countless hours swimming with his buddies and also served as a baptismal pool for my grandmother. We drove to the site where my grandfather had a grocery story and the little country church where my ancestors worshipped and the neighboring cemetery where they were buried.

Those places are etched in my mind. Dad's drives helped me understand my dad, his way of thinking, his vision and dreams for his children. Through those sites I saw his undying love for God and his family of the past, present and future.

Dad's "heritage drives" were a blessing and well worth the trip.

—Georgia Curtis Ling

The Turning Point

"Mom? Are you in the kitchen?" Suzanne, my 14-year-old daughter, called as she slammed the front door. After rummaging through the refrigerator, she turned to face me.

"You and Dad each have to write a letter to me," she said. "Fr. Keen said we have to bring them with us to the retreat."

The thought of a letter to my daughter made me feel uneasy. We were a busy family. My husband and I both worked outside our home, and evening hours were spent overseeing homework, cleaning the house, cooking balanced meals, and tending to outside chores.

That evening, I told my husband about the upcoming retreat for Suzanne's entire class. "We each have to write a letter to her that she'll open and read while she's there," I added.

My husband dropped his newspaper and stared at me. "A letter? To Suzanne? It seems a little foolish . . . embarrassing," he said.

The next evening my husband sat at the kitchen table with a pad of paper before him. He seemed deep in thought as he rolled the pen back and forth between his hands. Not normally demonstrative, I knew this was difficult for him.

As for me, I went to the typewriter. Suddenly, I realized that I was only accustomed to issuing orders, complaining about unfinished chores, and making threats about cluttered bedrooms. What did I honestly want to say to Suzanne? More importantly, what did she need to hear?

I closed my eyes and thought of Mary, Jesus' mother. What would she say if she were writing this letter?

I started. "Fourteen years ago, when the nurse placed you in my arms, I was so happy! A daughter! Then my other responsibilities began distracting me. I've been too busy cooking to tell you how proud I am of you. I've been too busy . . ."

Words soon filled the page.

My inhibitions had dissolved. I wrote what I truly felt. I stuck with honest feelings and made no corrections. I signed off with "Always remember that I love you," put the letter into an envelope, and tucked it her suitcase. Her father's letter, in a separate sealed envelope, was placed next to mine.

When Suzanne returned from the retreat, she hugged us and said, "I love you both. Thanks." No further explanations were necessary. We knew our letters were filled with words that were long overdue.

—Lois Erisey Poole

Just Beyond The Curtain

When the phone rang loudly at 4:55 A.M., I knew it was Tammy. I was going to be a gramma!

As Bob and I hurried to the hospital, I couldn't help thinking how different things were today than when Tammy had arrived twenty-four years earlier. I had been put into a small room and left alone; only a nurse checked in on my progress periodically. Then when the time arrived, I was wheeled forty miles an hour down a long corridor to the room where babies were delivered—without husband or relatives near.

I was excited at the thought of being allowed in the birthing room with Tammy and Rod. How special this time would be for us. As we drove through the silent night, I thought of all the things I would do to make the time more comfortable for my daughter.

I rushed into the room and found her well cared for by capable nurses. Rod's masculine hand held Tammy's tiny one as he lovingly put a damp washcloth on her sweaty brow. "You're doing fine," his deep voice assured her.

His dark brown eyes met mine and I knew that Tammy didn't need me any more. Giving her an encouraging smile and a hearty thumbs up, I slowly backed out the door and stood in the hallway outside the room.

This was their time: hers and Rod's. It was time for me to realize Tammy was no longer my little girl. She was a mother herself. A grown woman with someone else to take care of her from now on. The lump in my throat was hard to swallow, but I thanked God that Rod was the responsible, reliable person he was.

Bob and I stood outside the curtain with Linda and Sam, Rod's parents, awaiting the first little cry. It came at 10:02 A.M. and I thanked God for another life coming into this world.

It's hard to let go. To suddenly become aware that our children no longer need us. I thought back to the day of Tammy's birth.

How I held her tiny little hand and prayed for the strength I knew I would need to raise her.

Please, Lord, guide this new mother and father as they start out on the long road of parenthood. Make them aware of Your presence and Your love. And help me to always be there, Father, just beyond the curtain, to offer advice when asked, love when needed and understanding when times seem impossible to face alone.

—Marcia Krugh Leaser

If I Had My Child To Raise Over Again

If I had my child to raise all over again,

I'd finger paint more, and point the finger less.

I'd do less correcting, and more connecting.

I'd take my eyes off my watch, and watch with my eyes.

I would care to know less, and know to care more.

I'd take more hikes and fly more kites.

I'd stop playing serious, and seriously play.

I'd run through more fields, and gaze at more stars.

I'd do more hugging, and less tugging,

I would be firm less often, and affirm much more.

I'd build self-esteem first, and the house later.

I'd teach less about the love of power,

And more about the power of love.

—Diane Loomans

Boy Adjustments

My first grandchild was a noisy, active little boy. After raising three daughters, this was an entirely new experience for me. I didn't realize just what an adjustment little Matthew had been until one morning when my daughter was visiting and I overheard her saying, "Matthew you had better settle down today. We haven't even had breakfast yet and Grandma has already thanked God three times for giving her daughters!"

—June Cerza Kolf

DRENCHED IN THE SPIRIT

RECENTLY my seven-year old son was baptized at nearby Lake Tahoe. With tears streaming down my face, I watched as he came out of the water, then excitedly asked if he felt any different. "Yeah, Mom, I do," he replied. "Now I have water up my nose!"

—Leslie A. Williamson

6

Friendship

You shall love the LORD your God with all your heart, with all your soul, with all your strength, and with all your mind, and your neighbor as yourself.

Luke 10:27

Prepare A Place

Mary Kay and I were inseparable ever since that scary day when I flung my skinny, nine-year-old frame between her and the big Boxer who periodically broke loose to terrorize the neighborhood.

"Two peas in a pod," teased our parents.

As youngsters, we spent rainy days indoors playing Monopoly or Chinese Checkers. Sometimes we played something more imaginative, like Hollywood movie stars complete with costumes. When we played "movie star," I was the gregarious Carmen Miranda with a makeshift fruit bowl atop my head while Mary Kay was the more demure type like Scarlet O'Hara posing with hankie in hand.

But the imagination of our childhood never could fathom that one childhood episode in particular would later come to parallel a sad adult drama. It began one winter day when we were sledding down the snow covered hills the park district set aside for that purpose.

Suddenly skidding out of control, I flew head first into a staunch old Dutch Elm tree. At the sight of my bleeding forehead Mary Kay carried on as though I had died. When I chided her for over reacting, she wailed with typical teenage dramatics: "Whatever would I do if anything happened to you?"

The parallel to this escapade developed shortly after we entered what we promised would be our personal "fabulous forties." One chilly October night, the phone interrupted my work on Halloween costumes for my four children. It was Mary Kay's husband, Jimmy. He was very upset, but managed to stammer: "We rushed Kay to the hospital. She's in a coma. it doesn't look good. Better get here fast."

On the way to the hospital, panic stirred up the usual mix of denial that so often tortures those in the throes of shock:

"Kay can't be dying. She's never even been sick. And please God, she's only forty-two years old. No one dies at forty-two. Besides, I'm the one who always goes first on our adventures."

As I drew close to the interstate exit ramp, a host of experiences we shared in our growing years flooded my thoughts.

There was the summer we were gangly fourteen-year-olds, and convinced we were old enough to swim in the deep water at the park pool, we headed in. But an angry lifeguard hauled us out, with an order that park rules required us to first prove we could swim across the deep end, twice, non-stop.

Being the older of the two, I usually went first on any new adventure. After successfully completing my swim, I leaned over the pool's edge screaming encouragement as Mary Kay struggled with the final laps: "Keep kicking! If you give up he won't let you stay here with me!"

Nearing the hospital parking lot, more memories bombarded my troubled mind like the times we comforted each other through our failed adolescent romances; and how we giggled wildly while trying to teach our baseball buddies a simple two-step for the high school prom. Or how I again went first when we entered the adult working world, boasting to my boss about Mary Kay: "She's responsible, prompt, tidy and talented."

We went on to witness our weddings, await the birth of babies, and weep when Mary Kay remained childless. But that just gave her reason to love mine more. "Aunty Kay always brings those great store-bought birthday cakes," marveled my children bored by my home decorated disasters.

These treasured memories helped calm me during the race to the hospital. But when I reached Mary Kay's bedside, the sight of her so stiff and helpless lost in a maze of tubes and wires, retriggered the panic. The unexpected aneurysm had burst inside her brain doing total damage. Only one wayward curl wiggling out of the edge of a head bandage, alluded to the lively young woman now cloaked in silence.

"Whatever will I do without you?" I groaned.

Leaning closer, I whispered over and over words that I hoped would be the key to unlock the door of that secret place the coma had carried her so that she could hear me coaching her back like that day at the pool many years ago.

"Keep kicking, Kay! I'm here for you!"

But after a long while and too many tears, I accepted that this time it was Mary Kay who went first. And until God deemed it time for me to follow, I was sure Mary Kay would be busy preparing a place for me on this . . . our ultimate adventure.

—Jean Rodgers

"For an extra $25, Ruth here will crouch behind you and tug on the back of your scalp so it'll look like you've had a facelift."

Little Things Mean A Lot

A "million" years ago when I was a teenager, I was "sure" I would never be pretty, never have a date and certainly never get married. I disliked most of my features, hated my curly hair, and was convinced I was fat. However, my feet were definitely my worst feature. I tried to keep them out of sight at all times. There is a picture of me at an eighth grade function with my toes turned up in a most peculiar position—a futile attempt to shorten them! It didn't occur to me that such a contortion would only draw attention to what I wished to hide. They were big. At thirteen, I reluctantly stood up in size 9's.

As time passed, I came to accept myself and even my feet. Maturity and a lot of encouraging words from family and friends helped me learn to properly evaluate my looks and put them in proper perspective.

And some of those encouraging words came from a completely unexpected source. Every high school has at least one boy who is every teenage girl's ideal. We called them "dreamboats." I think today's dreamboat is called a hunk.

Ronnie was ours. I had admired him from afar since the sixth grade. It was the Spring of my senior year and I had summoned the courage to wear an eye-catching pair of white ballet slippers. The bus was crowded as Ronnie got on. Surveying his choices, he sauntered down the aisle and casually dropped beside me, favoring me with his devastating, lopsided grin. And then his eyes fell to my feet. I have no idea what prompted his words but I have never forgotten them: "You've got pretty feet, Nance."

Thirty years ago and I still treasure those words! Just casual words from a popular boy to a girl who was not.

I wonder what casual remark of mine someone carries around? Is it a kind compliment like Ronnie's or an off-the-cuff statement that wounded and rewounded for years?

Little things mean a lot.

—**Nancy L. Goodwin**

Everyone Needs Someone

People need people and friends need friends
And we all need love for a full life depends
Not on vast riches or great acclaim,
Not on success or on worldly fame,
But just in knowing that someone cares
And holds us close in their thoughts and prayers—
For only the knowledge that we're understood
Makes everyday living feel *wonderfully good*,
And we rob ourselves of life's greatest need
When we "lock up our hearts" and fail to heed
The outstretched hand reaching to find
A kindred spirit whose heart and mind
Are lonely and longing to somehow share
Our joys and sorrows and to make us aware
That life's completeness and richness depends
On the things we share with our loved ones and friends.

—Helen Steiner Rice

Unscheduled Flight

I had some nifty refrigerator magnets made up with these words from Konrad Lorenz: "Heartily laughing together at the same thing forms an immediate bond." So true! When we've shared a big laugh together, some invisible walls have come down between us, and we've taken our relationship one step higher.

Comedians always begin, "Have you heard the one about . . ." Well, I know you haven't heard this one, because only two women in the world know it happened (When you finish reading this, there will be three of us!)

I had just walked into the passenger terminal at the Indianapolis airport and was looking for somewhere to sit until they called my flight. Almost every seat was filled. At the end of one of the rows were two seats joined together on a T-shaped base. On one of those seats sat a very thin young lady who barely took up half of her side. "Perfect!" I thought, heading toward the other vacant side.

I sat down carefully, smiled at her, and began to arrange my packages around me. As I was leaning over to close my briefcase, this little slip of a woman apparently stood up. Unfortunately, she was my ballast.

Seconds later, I was shouting out something like, "G-r-r-a-a-a-a-k-k!" I turned the entire double seat completely over sideways and I went tumbling, tails over teacups. Needless to say, this attracted the attention of the men at the ticket counter, who rushed over to help.

They couldn't get me off the floor. Not because of my size (after all, there were three of them), not because I was pinned under the chair, but because I was laughing too hard. All my muscles were so relaxed I was like a large, limp Raggedy Ann doll on roller skates.

They kept asking me, "Are you okay, Miss? Are you okay? Shall we call a doctor?" Well, that made me laugh harder, until I was almost gasping for air. Finally, they helped me get to a standing position and steered me toward the seat, back on its T-shaped feet again. I very carefully sat down in the middle of the T and took a deep breath.

Assuring everyone around me that I was just fine, I began to pull my coat together and stuff some things back into my carry-on bag. Every few seconds, I had to stifle another giggle. Pulling out a small mirror to check and see if my lipstick had survived my unscheduled "flight," I caught a glimpse of another large woman seated near me who was watching me with great interest. Her lips were so pinched together, she looked like she had swallowed a large cat.

I sized her up as a "sister" immediately, leaned over to her and whispered, "I'm just thankful I didn't flip that little woman up in the air."

That was all it took. This woman exploded with the loudest "H-a-a-a-w-w-w-w!" I've ever heard, before or since. Having just barely recovered myself, I was right in there with her, howling and snorting and slapping my knee. People would not even look in our direction.

I may never see her again, but that woman and I are now joined at the funny bone for life!

—Liz Curtis Higgs

My Daughter, My Friend

Dear Mother, the letter began. *Happy Mother's Day! I truly hope this is a happy day for you! I wanted so much to be able to send you something nice and slightly expensive, but I can't afford to. Now that I am a mature woman and the mother of four, I know how you must have felt many times. I am sure you wanted to give us things you couldn't afford . . . or maybe just take us to the dentist more often, etc.*

My mind went back to the birth of Barbara. She was our fourth child following three sons. We were overjoyed. A sister was born just one day after Barbara's first birthday, making our family complete. With five children, there were indeed times when our money didn't go far enough!

> *Thank you for loving me when I was most unlovable, for worrying about me, and for the sacrifices you made for me. Most of all, Mom, I thank you for every godly quality you faithfully modeled.*

We had tried to raise our children for Christ. They were involved in church activities from the time they were very young. Barbara had shown a tender heart from the beginning, yet kept many of her thoughts and feelings to herself. As she grew older, there were the usual patterns of adolescent rebellion. She often treated us as if we were poison when we would touch her or her belongings, using a make-believe can of spray as a disinfectant.

She made a decision to go her own way early in her teen years. During the baby-sitting years, we found out Barbara was sneaking behind our backs and smoking. The woman she baby-sat for was supplying her with cigarettes. I remember well the wedge that was driven between us when we no longer allowed her to care for the two little boys of whom she had become so fond.

During her high school senior year, Barbara talked of moving out so that she could be free to do "her own thing." I told her we could not give our permission until after she graduated and had a regular job. Then, I promised, we would be happy to help her move. She angrily answered, "You will never cut the apron strings!"

Following graduation, Barbara did find a job and soon located an apartment. She even took me to see it. I approved of her choice, although I was not happy with the girls she had chosen as housemates.

The day she moved, I presented her with a gift-wrapped pair of starched, ironed apron strings from one of my favorite aprons. The strings were wrapped with the following letter:

Dear Barbara,

As you can see, the apron strings have been cut! I regret that the past few years have been filled with so much conflict. Be assured that the decisions your father and I have made were for your best interests. Perhaps you will understand when you have a teenage daughter of your own.

Your future decisions are your own. If mistakes are made, you will suffer the consequences. You are free to "do your own thing." God is the only one you have to answer to.

We will be here if you need us, but will not interfere if you do not ask. If joys are experienced, we will rejoice with you. When sorrow comes to you, we will hurt with you as well.

Our constant prayers will be that you will find God's best for your life in whatever you do. We love you very much!

Mom and Dad

The promises I made in my letter were tested. I will never forget the day Barbara told us she was pregnant. How our hearts ached for and with her. However, we confirmed our love for her and supported her. We continued to pray. Communication lines seemed to be more open.

In time, we were thrilled when Barbara became so tired of sin that she called upon God and became a Christian. What a change He has brought in her heart and life!

Thank you for being my mother and for helping me to be a good mother (and woman). I have learned from your good points and from your mistakes, and I hope my children will learn from mine. My children are my passion.

My mind drifted back to a phone call shortly after Barbara was saved. When I answered the phone, she burst into tears. She asked my forgiveness for the way she had treated me during those growing-up years. She told me her own 10-year-old daughter had just lashed out at her, saying some very hurtful things. Barbara had been forcefully reminded of her responses to me, and was deeply repentant, knowing they had hurt me deeply.

Now I understand what it means to be a mother and what it means to be loved by a wonderful mother like you! I will never be able to say thank you enough for all that you have done for me. I really do love you, Mom.

Your daughter,
Barbara

As I finished Barbara's Mother's Day letter, tears of joy ran down my face. Barbara and I now share a closeness we had never before experienced. I can truthfully say, "Through Christ, my daughter became my friend!"

—Virginia Baty

T Is For Tammy

"The Tin Grin Is In"—was what the T shirt boasted, and my youngest daughter had inherited it from her older sister on the day she got her braces. The braces were new, she wore them for two years. The T shirt wasn't . . . she wore it for two years also.

We used to practically have a war when I'd want to wash it. Somehow it never looked as if I'd won.

"Do you tie that thing to your bed post at night so it won't run away?" I'd tease.

"Nope, I wear it under my pajamas," she would grin. "Just kidding," she'd add with a shiny smile.

That old T-shirt was a lot like Tammy herself; sort of hung loose, but always there when needed.

"T is for Tammy, and T-shirt." she would say proudly, "And don't worry, Mom, some day I'll grow up and won't want it anymore."

I sighed a heavy sigh, wishing that day would be soon.

Sometimes I would cringe, as she'd run out of the house wearing her jeans with the knees out, her red bandanna tied around one thigh, her jean jacket with the sleeves cut off (the cuffs from them around her bare wrists) and, of course, the T-shirt.

"I'm making a statement," she would say boldly.

I wasn't sure I was glad or sad. I didn't know what Tammy was trying to say.

The months passed and Tammy grew in grace and beauty. Suddenly her room was filled with posters and her radio was tuned to whatever station was the loudest. The braces were replaced by a retainer and the sleeveless jean jacket hung unworn in her closet. Tammy was growing up.

All this sort of slipped by, unnoticed—until today. I found the T-shirt in the things to be thrown away. I'd been praying for this day for two years. Then could someone please explain to me why, as I saw it lying there in a crumpled heap . . . I cried?

—Marcia Krugh Leaser

Fun Is Where You Find It

I have learned to find fun in unlikely places. Fun is a mystery. You cannot trap it like an animal; you cannot catch it like the flu. But it comes without bidding, if you are looking for it.

Recently I made a sad trip—by plane to Michigan for the funeral of a beloved aunt. As I boarded my return flight to California, I noticed a little black girl, sitting all hunched up across the aisle from me. She looked so small and so afraid. The flight attendant told me she was traveling alone.

I thought, *Oh, well, the attendants will look after her.* I was busy going over the last few days . . . the funeral . . . the many people who had grown older since I had last seen them . . . it was all very depressing. I knew the five-hour flight home would be my only time to be alone with my loss. I had no intention of entertaining a little six-year-old who evidently had never been on a plane before.

As the plane took off, I noticed that she shut her eyes tightly and clenched the seat belt with bone-white knuckles. I felt something inside me want to ask her to come sit by me.

When we were safely in the air, I asked the attendant if it was all right, and she replied, "Oh, yes! She has never flown before. Her parents have divorced, and she's on her way to California to live with relatives she's never met before. Thank you for caring."

My "fun" started when the hostess came through with the complimentary beverages. Darling, little Suzie with her dancing black eyes said she would have a 7-Up. I asked the hostess to put it in a fancy glass, with a cherry in it, because we were pretending we were special VIP ladies taking a super trip. Having 7-Up with a cherry in it in a fancy glass may not be your idea of fun, but to a six-year-old who had never had it that way before, it was great fun. We were off to a great start.

Our pretending went on, and I could see that I had missed so much in having all boys, never learning as a mother of a girl what little girls thought of. Suzie thought the luncheon on the plane was just like miniatureland. The tiny salt containers were a great joke. The tiny cup from the salad dressing was just for Munchkins. I had so much fun, enjoying with her child's eyes, all the goodies on our trays. We had our own special tea party. The little paper umbrella anchored in the dessert caused her to remark, "I got to see *Mary Poppins* once." I knew this was one of her most special experiences, and so we pretended that she was Mary Poppins. We kept her little umbrella, and Suzie had to learn to walk like Mary Poppins, with her toes sideways and holding the umbrella up just so. She did a great imitation!

Just taking Suzie to the little bathroom was an experience. She couldn't figure out how things worked. She wanted to know if the soap was so small because somebody had used it almost all up!

When we returned to our seats, the attendant gave us both coloring books and three crayons—blue, red, and yellow. So, together, we colored some puppies in the book red, made a yellow gypsy, and a blue ballerina. It was fun! She had lost her fear of flying, and we looked out on the cottony sea of clouds, talking about what fun it would be to walk on the clouds, holding our Mary Poppins umbrellas, and seeing how far we could go.

Then it was time to land. The hours had melted away. I had been a child for a few hours, playing her game, coloring her pictures, exploring her child's mind, seeing life through the eyes of six-year-old. I had learned so much!

I will always remember that fun day, and when I eat on an airline flight, I always think of the "Munchkin" dinner Suzie and I shared that day. She got off ahead of me when we landed, and I rushed to try to catch up with her. I saw as she was swooped up into the arms of a grandmotherly black lady with twinkles in her eyes. Suzie turned to me and said, "Look, Grandma, I am Mary Poppins!" She held her little umbrella up, turned her little feet sideways, and smiled a big smile of pure joy. The grandmother thanked me for looking after her, but I was the one who was taken care of that day!

It could have been a dreary, sad trip for me, lost in my own reverie of sorrow, but instead a little girl became a diamond of love and joy for me.

When life gets so heavy for you, and you wonder how you can cope with all the load, learn to put on the garment of joy for the spirit of heaviness, and fun is included in that garment of joy. Suzie turned my desert into a decorated place of joy. Look for that joy in your life, too. Don't settle for grouchiness and sorrow: settle for joy and happiness.

—Barbara Johnson

QUOTABLE QUOTES

WHILE attending an aunt's funeral, my four-year old son David, sat between his Uncle John and me. After reading John 3:16, the pastor noted it could be found in the Gospel according to John. Those around us smiled as David looked at his uncle and asked," Uncle John, did you really say that?"

—M. Doris Murphy

What Is Your Smile Worth?

It costs nothing, yet creates much.

It enriches those who receive it without impoverishing those who give.

It happens in a flash and the memory of it sometimes lasts *forever.*

No one is so wealthy that they can get along without it, and no one is so poor that they are not enriched by its benefits.

It creates happiness in the home, fosters good will in business, and is the countersign of friends.

It is rest to the weary, daylight to the discouraged, sunshine to the sad, and nature's best antidote for trouble.

And if, in the hurry and rush of the day, you meet someone who is too weary to give you a SMILE, leave one of yours.

For no one needs a smile so much as those who have none left to give!

—Unknown

7

God's Guidance

☆

The steps of a good man are ordered by the LORD: and he delighteth in his way.

Psalm 37:23

Imparting A Rich Spiritual Inheritance

Combing through the bookshelf at my parents house recently, I discovered an old book by the great evangelist D. L. Moody entitled *Wondrous Love*.

"I'll show it to Luis," I thought, knowing how much my evangelist husband would appreciate a collection of sermons by Moody.

On the inside cover, however, I found a surprise—an unexpected tribute to my spiritual heritage. My grandmother had given the book to my parents when I was born. On the flyleaf she wrote these words: "To Elsie and Willard on Patricia's first birthday. May her sweet little life be dedicated to Him whose wondrous love never fails—John 3:16. From Mother, June 24, 1937."

My parents weren't Christians. They avoided all conversations on religious subjects. But my grandparents had recently placed their faith in Jesus Christ. Of course, they wanted their children and grandchildren to experience that same new life.

My parents were less than enthused with the gift. But that didn't stop my grandparents from communicating, by word and by example, the good news of godly living. Within several years both my parents confessed the Lord Jesus as their Savior, and at age eight I did too.

The Gospel messages contained in *Wondrous Love* were preached during Moody's first mission to England. My grandmother didn't know that I would marry an evangelist and that we would invest much time preaching the Gospel in England. But the book she gave nearly 60 years ago will always be a precious token of God's faithfulness, because He rewarded her desire to impart a godly inheritance to her family.

God has no grandchildren. Each one of us must personally come to Christ. Nevertheless, I thank God for grandparents who affected me for eternal good. My parents' conversion, my own salvation, and the faith of my children stem back to my grandparents' prayers and godly example.

—**Pat Palau**

Angel Down

Several years ago my husband and I were driving home to our two-room apartment, discussing what we would need for our soon-to-be-born first baby.

"I'd like to get a baby quilt," I suggested.

"But, Honey, you know I'm just a bacteriology student on a summer job and our budget is strained by the bare necessities."

I knew he was right, but Matthew 6:28, 30 popped into my mind, "Why take ye thought for raiment? Consider the lilies of the field . . . If God so clothes the grass of the field . . shall He not much more clothe you?"

We rode along a few miles. Then I noticed something blue lying ahead of us on the road. We stopped, and running over to it, I realized it was a piece of blue cotton cloth. I also noticed some loose cotton nearby. There was just enough to make a baby quilt! I looked up and down the road, but there was no car in sight to account for the materials. It was as if an angel had thrown baby blanket materials down from the sky. I gathered it all up and within a few days had made a quilt from it with a pink cotton binding around its edges.

When my baby son arrived he lived only two days. Sadly, I put away the little quilt. Later the Lord blessed us with another baby and I covered her with the little quilt. When her little brother joined our household he was warmed by the small quilt, too. I have always called it my "angel quilt" for God provided for my babies' needs and it seems the materials were left there just for me.

—BettyRuth Stevens

Unseen Hand

When trouble overcomes me
And my heart sometimes cries,
An Unseen Hand is near
To brush tears from my eyes.

When I feel sad and lonely,
It's hard to understand
That love unconditional
Is a gift from an Unseen Hand.

At times I have wandered
Just like a shepherd's lamb,
Away from the love of God,
Away from the Unseen Hand.

But the Unseen Hand reaches out
And guides me toward His Throne,
Tenderly I hold my Father's hand —
No longer am I all alone.

—Nanette Thorsen-Snipes

Kindergarten Blues

"I just want to stay home like before. I don't have to go anymore. OK? While her jaw was set and her voice firm, Kelley, our five-year-old daughter knew it was *not* OK. She had already learned that some things in life were not options and school was one of them.

For days I dismissed Kelley's reluctance to go to kindergarten as nervous jitters brought on by a different environment, though I had not anticipated it. Our middle daughter looked forward to new experiences and was anything but timid. "I'm going to real school!" she had announced repeatedly all summer. But when her anxiety continued, even with prayer each morning before she left, I made an appointment with her teacher.

Kelley's teacher, Carol Winer, was a soft spoken lady who was also worried about Kelley's anxiety. As we talked, neither of us had answers. I left our meeting comforted only with the knowledge that we were both aware of the situation and we were both praying.

The next few weeks Kelley verbalized her unhappiness less, but it was apparent she felt miserable. I longed for the return of her spontaneous sense of humor and pixie grin, but each morning I continued to wake up a frowning little girl with tightly clenched fists.

One day when Kelley was dismissed from school, I thought I detected a glimmer of excitement in her clear blue eyes. By the time we reached our house, I knew all about Jason, the boy in the yellow shirt who sat next to Kelley at snack time, and about Lisa's father's new job and Jennifer's grandma coming to visit. What I wanted to know was, what had erased the fears and frustrations that had dominated our world for over a month? Nothing she said provided an answer.

At the dinner table that night, Kelley revealed the secret. "Know what happened at my school today?" she asked, exuberantly.

"No, what?" her dad replied.

"This little kid bumped into me and made me fall in the water under the slide. My teacher picked me up and said she was very sorry. She carried me to the bathroom and took off my shoes. They were muddy and my socks were muddy too." Her voice became soft but intense. "Then know what? She washed my feet."

All conversation paused. Kelley searched our faces, her wide eyes showing the impact of servanthood. Pools filled my eyes as I realized how God had answered our prayers.

Christ humbly bathed the tired and dirty feet of His disciples, ignoring his position of authority and adopting the attitude of a slave. Though they didn't realize it at the time, His example would change the lives of His followers and those they ministered to. Without being aware, Mrs. Winer soothed Kelley's doubts and convinced her that she was cared for, by exercising this expression of servanthood.

—Patricia Smith

The Accusation

On the last night of a fall revival meeting at the small country church where my family and I attended when I was growing up, Paula, the pastor's daughter, played the invitational hymn "Softly and Tenderly" on the rickety piano.

She stopped at the end of the chorus, and I let out a deep breath. *Thank goodness that's over.* I couldn't have stood another day of unleashed jealousy because Paula could play the piano when I couldn't even sing. We were about the same size and age, but the similarity ended there.

My relief was short-lived. After the last "Amen," Paula ran to me and waved a five-dollar bill under my nose. "Look," she said bubbling, "Deacon Jones gave me this. I never expected to be paid for playing. Isn't it wonderful?"

I couldn't believe it. Our church, like the farmers in the area, was less than prosperous. We paid the Pastor only twenty-five dollars a month, and he drove his family fifty miles and back each Sunday. I burst out, "I don't believe you. I saw the deacon put the offering plate on top the piano. You took it, didn't you?"

Paula's eyes widened, and then she pressed her lips together and walked away.

My stomach scrunched into a tight ball. *Why did I say such a horrible thing?* I'd have felt better if Paula had slapped me. All the way home, I couldn't get the look on Paula's face out of my mind. Finally, I decided I'd tell Mama about it tomorrow and asked her what to do.

For the next two days I followed Mama around like a baby chick, trying to get up enough courage to talk to her about my problem but I couldn't. At bedtime, Mama came into my room, kissed me on the cheek and said, "Goodnight, sweet one."

I couldn't tell her then. If she knew what I'd done, she might not call me "sweet one" ever again, and I couldn't bear that. Mama left, and I sobbed into my pillow.

My guilt tormented me day and night. I decided I'd apologize to Paula on Sunday and forget the whole rotten mess. But the minute I saw Paula, something mean inside me took over. She wore a new blue dress with rickrack on the collar and sleeves, and a bright, blue ribbon adorned her new permanent wave.

Paula sat next to me as if nothing at all had happened. *She's deliberately being nice*, I thought. I forgot I'd resolved to apologize.

On the way home, Mama glanced back at me. "Didn't Paula look pretty in her new dress and hairdo? I'm so glad for her. 'Rejoice with them that do rejoice,' it says in the Bible." I felt so sad I couldn't reply.

School started the next day. It was my first year in high school, and I was so excited I soon believed I could forget my wrong-doing. Two other things happened that helped me block out the hurtful memory. We moved to another farm where we had a bathtub for the very first time, and Paula's dad resigned the pulpit because his ancient car quit running.

Soon, Mrs. Everly, who lived near the old farm, walked more than two miles to visit us. She held a handful of rags and a pint of kerosene. "Hello," she said, "I'm so glad you have a bathtub now. Would you let me clean it for you?"

She hurried into our bathroom with Mama and me at her heels. Astonished, I watched Mrs. Everly scour the tub with kerosene, then shine it until it looked like new snow in the sun. I could barely wait until she'd gone to ask Mama why.

Mama looked thoughtful. "She practices what the Bible says. Do you remember Romans 12:15, 'Rejoice with them that do rejoice'? Even if she doesn't have a bathtub, she's real glad we have one. That's her way of showing us."

I pondered Mama's words all afternoon. The awesome weight of last August's unfair accusation suddenly returned. Mama had quoted those same words from Romans the day she'd mentioned Paula's new dress and hairdo.

I decided Mama had known all along I coveted Paula's good fortune. She'd been trying to help me then just as she was now. I went to find Mama.

Mama was mixing cornbread, but she stopped when she saw my face and turned to me with outstretched arms. I ran to her and my tears splotched her apron. She hugged me and stroked my hair until I quieted, then I told her all about being jealous of Paula and accusing her of stealing the five dollars.

"Will God forgive me?" I whispered.

Mama kissed my tear-stained cheek. "Of course, sweet one."

Kneeling beside my bed I prayed for forgiveness, then gazed at my image in my mirror. *I could have saved myself alot of agony if I'd confessed immediately. It's strange. I still look like a twelve-year-old—but I feel so much older and wiser today.*

—Doris C. Crandall

The Tomato Parable

During my formative years, our church had one of the best youth programs to be found anywhere. We had regular Saturday night praise and worship meetings for young people. There were bonfires and testimony times on the beach, and there were wonderful youth revivals in the summer. Teams of the brightest and best young preachers from Universities and Seminaries came to lead two-week "youth revivals." After the services, we met for refreshments, and then we got to ask questions of the revivalists: those gorgeous, gifted, intense young "preacher boys." One recurring question had to do with "petting" or "making out." For Baptist young people, those were the burning issues in the forties, along with dancing.

One young Baylor preacher explained, "Let me tell you a story about the farmer's market I visited recently. There was a bushel of tomatoes sitting out front where everyone could squeeze them to test for ripeness. Those poor tomatoes were bruised and split, and flies circled all over them. However, inside the market was a display case with lovely tomatoes under the glass. They were glistening clean, fresh and dewy."

He paused dramatically to let us all visualize the story; then he continued. "When I choose a wife, I want one of those clean tomatoes kept under glass!"

We all got the message! All of us wanted to be his tomato!

Soon, I had a date with a handsome hunk named Donny. By then, my family had returned to the farm so he had to drive the eight miles out into the hills to pick me up. Mama didn't like his looks at all, so Mama and Daddy, along with grandma McClure held an impromptu prayer meeting for "Kathryn Jane."

Meanwhile, at the movies, Donny behaved fairly well. But after the feature film, instead of heading for Field's Cafe where the high school and college crowd hung out, he headed for the

Old River Road. I knew what was on his mind; he never guessed I had tomatoes on mine.

As we drove through the darkness, my brain was spinning! *How can I get out of this situation gracefully?* I prayed my usual emergency prayer: "Lord! Lord!" and suddenly, had an epiphany! Every devout Baptist child learns early on how to "witness," so, as Donny drove up and down the Washita Valley looking for a place to park, I talked to him about his eternal salvation. Finally, after my mouth was dry and I'd exhausted my considerable repertoire of Bible verses, Donny sighed and headed for my home. When I let myself into the house just before midnight, Mama, Papa and Grandma were still praying.

Twenty-three years later, I heard from Donny again. He was a steward in his Methodist Church and often led lay witness missions. Of course, it may not be true, but I've liked to claim some credit for that—or was it my family's prayers that night? Or perhaps that young preacher boy, the purveyor of the tomato parable, will get another star in his crown?

—Dr. Kathryn Presley

A Hedge Of Protection

I had been enjoying my jog that Saturday afternoon as I listened to a worship tape on my yellow Walkman. I left about 4:30 p.m. from my parents home in a suburb of Las Vegas. I'd decided to go down a dirt road nearby, where a couple of guys were riding all-terrain vehicles. After I reached the end of the dirt road, I turned around to head back home.

As I ran, I felt enveloped in God's goodness. I had been struggling with bulimia and for the first time in many years I saw progress. God had brought me here to Las Vegas to pour out His grace and heal me from that terrible bondage. I was becoming free at last!

Suddenly out of nowhere, a man threw his arm around my neck from behind and jerked my head down to his hip. "Let go of me!" I shouted, as fear and panic overwhelmed me. As he dragged me off the road into the desert, I sensed the Lord speak gently to my heart, "I will be a wall of fire around you and a hedge of protection."

After a few feeble attempts to get free, I realized there was no way I could break his powerful grip. My body felt like an overcooked piece of linguini. So I began to pray out loud to God for His help. "Lord Jesus," I cried out, "Deliver this man from the stronghold of Satan. Convict him, Father, of his sinfulness and draw him close to You." I never would have imagined having compassion towards a man who was trying to harm me. But I felt that God had totally taken over in my weakness.

I had never before nor since felt God's presence so strongly. It was as if there were three huge angels surrounding me and I thought of the scripture in Psalm 91:11, "For He will give his angels charge concerning you, to guard you in all your ways."

I lifted up my hands and began to worship God. The stranger immediately stopped even though he had already taken off my clothes! He pulled me close to his chest and I began to share the

Gospel of salvation and forgiveness through Christ Jesus. "Do you feel a need for forgiveness?" I inquired. It wasn't difficult to convince him that he was not "basically a good person" under the circumstances. We talked for a few more minutes as I felt God leading.

Suddenly I felt like I had awakened from a bad dream. Reality hit me. I was in the middle of the desert outside Las Vegas witnessing to a rapist. I didn't know whether he had a weapon or if he intended to kill me. But I knew that my parents would be worried about me and that I needed to get home. "I'll tell you what," I said, "You take off in that direction and when you re gone I will gather my things and go in the other."

He sheepishly followed my instructions.

That traumatic experience built my faith and helped me to see His awesome power and love towards me. Not even a sparrow falls to the ground that escapes His notice, how much more does He keep His eye on His beloved children.

Since then the Ninety First Psalm has been very precious to me. I realize that though God chose to protect me from the evil intent of that man, there are many others who are violated every day in even more devastating ways. But God uses both experiences to bring about His will and His character in our lives. And it is comforting to know that He will never give us more than He knows we can handle.

—**Christie L. Qualls**

Breaking The News

Pamela Ashby of Ventura, California, says that when her aunt's beautiful dog suddenly died, the woman tried to break the news gently to her daughter, 5.

"We can all be happy now," Pamela concluded, "That Frisky is up in heaven with God."

"But mom," replied her daughter, "What's God going to do with a dead dog?"

—Unknown

Lost & Found

Sign Seen In A Doctor's Office:
I am lost!
I have gone to look for myself.
If I should return before I get back, please ask me to wait.
Thank you!

—**Unknown**

DIVINE REVELATION

WHEN my daughter lost her last baby tooth, I was weary of the Tooth Fairy and decided it was time to dispel this childhood myth. "Kelli," I said, "You know how the Easter Bunny is really Mommy, and Santa Clause is, too?" "Yes," she replied, a bit warily. "Well, there's one more person who really is me. Can you guess who that is?" Slowly , Kelli's eyes grew as big as saucers and her mouth dropped open. In a small, awe-filled voice, she said, "God?"

—Ellen Yinger

Love

We love, because He first loved us.

I John 4:19

Letting Go

My mother, with four children to raise as a single parent, ran a boarding house. It seemed only natural to her that I, the eldest, should get a degree in hotel and restaurant management to be better equipped to help in the business. After a year of those miserable courses, I told Mom if I couldn't major in journalism, I might as well drop out of college. From the time I'd begun reporting news on the Girl Scouts for our local newspaper, writing had been my love.

I reasoned with Mom that since I was working two jobs to pay my college tuition, I wanted to choose my own major. Thankfully, she agreed, and lived long enough to see me win the prestigious *Guideposts Magazine* writing contest, but not long enough to see my first book in print. I've always been grateful that she didn't insist on manipulating my career choice, and I've tried to follow her example with my own children.

—Quinn Sherrer

Duct Tape

"Leave it to my dad to hold everything together with duct tape," Mary exclaimed. "To him, duct tape was something like chicken soup; it could cure the ills of whatever was loose, crooked, wobbly, or otherwise viewed as broken. There was duct tape on the cabinets, duct tape on the chairs, duct tape on the dashboard, and even duct tape on his shoes."

Mary and I had a good laugh because, like her's, my dad liked to fix things too. But although the needy item again served its purpose, it was never quite the same after he finished rigging bobby pins, bits of wire, twisted paper clips, and yes, duct tape, to it. Mom would always try to call a repairman before Dad realized something needed attention. Once Dad got to it, you could never be sure what the face of the repair would look like. And it was always interesting to operate his new, improved contraption, because of course, there was some special way the item had to now be handled.

I'll never forget the back yard gate. The latch looked pretty simple to fix. One trip to the hardware store would have meant the acquisition of the necessary, identical parts. But, oh no. "Why waste the gas and the money on manufactured parts that are overpriced and poorly made?" he would query. "I've got everything I need to fix that latch right in the garage." We knew we were in trouble.

When Dad finished with the gate, you would have to balance on your right foot, hold the bottom of the gate steady with your left foot, while you lifted the latch a little with one hand and unwrap the wire around the post with the other. All of this had to be accomplished while the dog tried to escape the confines of the yard. We shuddered every time we had to use that gate, but Dad's feelings would have been hurt if we had changed it or criticized his effort.

I've learned a lot about fathers from remembering Mary's and my dad and their fascination with fixing things. Fathers carry the responsibility of everyone else in the family on their shoulders. It's because of their keen sense of that responsibility that they feel the need to fix whatever needs mending—from rickety fences, to torn shoes, to broken hearts. In our sophisticated society though, we've "advanced" to a level that makes us feel, "Who needs Dad to fix the really important things anymore?" We run to therapists, job counselors, and discovery groups to handle the things that trouble us. Dad's role as provider, protector, and fixer-upper has been stolen from him and we've lost out.

My dad passed away three years ago, but the back yard gate still has the same combination of wire and bits of string as it did when he first rigged it up. It stands as a reminder of his strength—the duct tape that held our family together. Dad's advice and counsel may not have been the most current, it might not have sounded snazzy or have cost 100 bucks an hour, but he tried the best he could to fix things with the only duct tape he could use on our emotions—the duct tape of love. It worked.

—Sharon Jones

The Words Of A Dummy

As a ventriloquist, I see God use my "dummy" Ezra in many different ways. At one of my speaking engagements, I saw a "dummy" cure one who wouldn't talk and one who felt ugly.

The Plaza in Portland, Oregon, is a graduated care facility. There they have a convalescent section called the Health Care Center. The lady in charge of the vespers asked if I could spend a few minutes in the Center. *No problem,* I figured. *I can do an easy 15 minute program.* Well, God had other things in mind.

With about 15 people there, in all stages of disability—many in wheel chairs, and several unable to tell me their names, I realized that a "program" was out of the question. The best thing was to have Ezra visit with each individual. What a joy it was to see these dear people respond to Ezra as he stood on their knees and talked to them.

But then we got to Katie, who is a tiny woman. She doesn't have a tooth in her head, but she has the sweetest face. There she sat in her wheelchair, all bundled in pink, holding a small teddy bear.

She was looking down when I approached her. But when I stood Ezra on her knees and he said, "Merry Christmas, Katie. I love you!" Katie lifted her head and her eyes lit up. She gave Ezra the most beautiful toothless grin I've ever seen. Ezra and Katie then began to carry on a rather animated conversation. I was trying to keep my focus on Katie, but was aware that something was going on with the staff. They were jumping up and down, hugging each other, laughing and crying at the same time. It wasn't until a few minutes later that I found out why. Katie hadn't talked in years! But there she was . . . talking a "blue streak" with Ezra.

Then there was Ada. Not as sweet looking as Katie. In fact, with rotting teeth, a slight drool, a whiskery chin, and disheveled hair, Ada actually was a bit homely. She kept bending down to stroke the legs of her chair, or she would pat herself. She too was in her own world. But each time Ezra would come to her she would stop the motions, then hold onto Ezra as she smiled and laughed, making her face light up with delight. In her delight, God let me see a special kind of beauty. I'm so grateful He did. As I stood Ezra on her knees, I had no idea that Ezra's simple words of "Ada, you is beautiful!" would have such a tremendous impact.

As soon as Ezra told her she was beautiful, Ada looked at him with stunned disbelief. "I'm beautiful! Oh! Do you really think I'm beautiful?" And when Ezra truthfully responded, "Yes, Ada, you is *real* beautiful. Merry Christmas!" Ada gave him a hug and her tears began to flow. Then she held him back, looked at him with a truly beautiful smile as she said with laughter, "Oh yes, it *is* a Merry Christmas. I'm *beautiful!*" As far as I was concerned, I had the richest Christmas ever!

—Gail Wenos

Squatter's Rights

One summer my 14-year-old niece, Keri, came to spend a week with me. She admired my wardrobe. "You spend a lot of money on your clothes, don't you?" she asked.

I smiled. "No. I make most of them myself."

Keri's eyes lit up. "Oh, please teach me to sew," she said. "There'll be plenty of time."

I sat down. "Ah, youth," I thought, "The *now* generation. A week? Impossible!" But the eagerness in her face won me over.

"We'll start with a cotton apron," I said. "Cotton's easy to sew."

Keri's face fell. "Please, Aunt Doris, I don't need an *apron*. Let's make a dress like this one." She held my latest quiana cloth creation up and whirled around in front of the mirror. "Only in pale purple. It'll go great with my hair and eyes. I'll wear it to church next Sunday."

To be able after years of practice, to make a dress of undisciplined quiana cloth is no great accomplishment. But to teach a youngster how to do it in a week's time—well, to me, those two feats are yards apart. But I relented.

Keri chose a dress pattern with a full-flared, gored skirt. That meant a lot of seams. We found orchid quiana at Cloth World, and I had to admit, as she draped the material over one shoulder, it did complement her long blond hair and green eyes.

Early Tuesday morning, I fit the pattern pieces to Keri. A near-perfect fit. I cleared the dining-room table and unfolded my cutting board across it. I showed Keri how to place and pin the pattern pieces on the material exactly as the pattern instructed.

With scissors poised, Keri said, "I'm nervous about cutting into this pretty cloth." *She's* nervous? My palms were sweaty. Nevertheless, Keri did a fair job. She sheared off only six notches, and I marked their places with chalk.

"Do I have to *bast* the seams?" Keri asked, as we resumed the lesson after lunch.

"That's *baste*," I said. "Absolutely. And sew all the seams in the direction indicated on the pattern. Skirt seams from bottom to top."

"Which is the bottom?" Keri asked.

At day's end my patience was threadbare. Keri didn't know a placket from a gusset, the pattern had both, and I wasn't good at explanations.

The next morning I got out the ironing board. "Are you going to iron?" Keri asked. "I thought you'd help me work on my dress." I showed her how to press open the seams, and thought she could handle that alone—so I dashed out for hamburger makings.

As I walked back into the kitchen, a triangular hole in the dress skirt gaped at me from the ironing board like a huge, irreverent eye.

Keri was crying. "You shouldn't have left me alone."

I grabbed a swatch, and we hurried to Cloth World. But the orchid-colored bolt was gone. My heart thumped to my stomach and gave me a queasy feeling.

"I sold it this morning," the clerk said, "All but a scrap. I thought I'd make a pillow cover."

The clerk must have seen my despair; I was too upset to hide it. "If it's enough for your use, I'll let you have it," she added.

Keri opened the car door for me. "I was so embarrassed," she mumbled.

"I'm sorry," I said.

The piece was barely enough to cut a new skirt section. I decided to stick to Keri like interfacing. Could this be only Wednesday afternoon?

To put it gently, we slashed out at each other often. But somehow by Saturday night we finished the dress. A miracle!

Twenty minutes before time for Sunday School Keri, radiant in her new dress, dashed from the bedroom and threw her arms around me.

"Thank you, Aunt Doris!" she exclaimed. Then she stepped back. "I feel sort of different inside. Do you think it's the dress?"

"Only partly," I replied through a lump in my throat, "Only partly."

Recently I read James Hilton's quotation, "If you forgive people enough, you belong to them and they to you, whether either person likes it or not—squatter's rights of the heart." After the trials of the week, Keri and I had forgiven each other so many times that we belonged to each other. We claimed squatter's rights of the heart.

—Doris C. Crandall

Am I A Real Grandma?

At the wedding, Melissa and her father held hands as they walked down the aisle. My daughter, Diana, was marrying Melissa's father, Mark. I had first met Melissa when she was two-and-a-half years old. A three foot tall blond with a freckled nose and bangs falling into large blue eyes that looked up at me.

"Hi, Melissa," I said.

"Are you Diana's mother?" she asked.

"Yes Melissa, I am." And with that she ran off to play. Since I lived more than 50 miles away from her, I believed there would be no opportunity to build a relationship. I wondered if it confused her when I was introduced to her as Grandma Irene. After all, she had two sets of biological grandparents already.

Six months after the wedding a phone call from Diana caused me some anxiety. She and Mark wanted to attend a wedding of a close friend near our home but needed someone to watch Melissa.

"Mom, would you baby-sit Melissa for an afternoon and evening while we attend the wedding?" Diana asked.

I hesitated. *I've never been a Grandma before. How do I do this? It's been many years since I was involved with young children and I haven't spent much time with Melissa.* But at last I agreed.

"Dear Lord," I prayed, "I don't know Melissa's likes or dislikes. I can only love her and pray for Your guidance that I will do the right thing."

Before the scheduled day arrived I purchased a supply of coloring books and crayons. I didn't know what else to buy, but it wasn't necessary because Melissa arrived carrying an armful of her own toys.

All the good-byes, hugs, and instructions from Diana and her dad completed, Melissa and I explored the house. She was a little shy at first but warmed up as I answered her questions. She decided to put her toys in the den next to the television.

Hesitantly I entered the den. *What do I do now?* "Come on Grandma, let's color in the coloring book." Her trust and acceptance eased my anxiety for the rest of the day. Melissa and I colored pictures, watched videos, and then went to play in the park. I pushed her on the swing until she spotted the rocket slide. She ran and jumped and made friends with the other children. After a time we were both tired. Me from watching and worrying and she from playing and running.

On the way home from the playground Melissa said she was hungry. "Grandma, may I have some spaghetti for dinner? Spaghetti is my favorite." We went to a local restaurant and ordered spaghetti. Melissa never stopped chattering in-between forkfuls of food. She talked about the trip to the park and all the different playground equipment. Even the waitress was charmed with her conversation and brought her a special dish of ice cream for dessert.

Melissa agreed with me we were both tired and full of food. We went home and lay on the sofa to watch cartoons on television and wait for Diana and her dad.

After some time they arrived and told us about the wedding. But there was no rest until Melissa told them all about the fun she had. When they were getting ready to leave, Melissa turned around, ran up to hug me and said, "I love you Grandma 'Rene. Thank you for a fun time."

"I love you too, Melissa, and may God bless you," I said as I choked back tears.

Lying in bed that night the events of the day replayed through my head. I thanked the Lord for all He had done to make it good. He opened the door for me to be a real Grandma.

—Irene Carloni

She Released Me

One day I traveled to Liverpool to tell my widowed mother that we were moving to the United States. Tears rolled down my cheeks when I saw her shock. When I heard her say, "How could you leave me?" I felt torn between the people I loved best—my mother and my husband. Then came an expression of the generous, giving, and sacrificial love so typical of her—"I'm sorry, Jill. How selfish of me. Of course you must go. Your place is at Stuart's side." We clung to each other, knowing she would never come to see us (she had an inordinate fear of flying), yet learning together once again the importance of release and sacrifice in love. When my time came to let go of our children, I was able to do so largely because my mother had taught me that you don't let go of a relationship—only your dependence on it. She had done it well, and for this and all the other things she and Dad did, I give thanks to God.

—**Jill Briscoe**

The Greatest Of These

My day began on a decidedly sour note when I saw my six-year-old wrestling with a limb of my azalea bush. By the time I got outside, he'd broken it.

"Can I take this to school today?" he asked.

With a wave of my hand, I sent him on. I turned my back so he wouldn't see the tears gathering in my eyes. I loved that azalea bush. I touched the broken limb to say silently, *I'm sorry.*

I wished I could have said that to my husband earlier, but I'd been angry. The washing machine had leaked on my brand-new linoleum. If only he'd taken the time to fix it the night before instead of playing checkers with Jonathan. *What are his priorities, anyway?*

I was still mopping up the mess on the floor when Jonathan followed me into the kitchen. "What's for breakfast, Mom?" he asked.

I opened the empty refrigerator. "Not cereal," I said, watching the sides of his mouth drop. "How about toast and jelly?" I smeared the toast with jelly and set it in front of him. *Why am I so angry?* I tossed my husband's dishes into the sudsy water. It was days like this that made me want to quit. I just wanted to drive my car up to the mountains, hide myself in a crevice, and never come down.

Somehow I managed to lug the wet clothes to the laundromat. I spent most of the day washing and drying clothes and thinking how love had disappeared from my life. Staring at the graffiti on the walls, I felt as wrung-out as the clothes left in the washers.

As I finished hanging up the last of my husband's shirts, I looked at the clock on the wall. *Oh no, I'm late to pick up Jonathan.* I dumped the clothes in the back seat and hurriedly drove to the school.

I was out of breath by the time I knocked on the teacher's door. I peered in through the glass. With one finger, she motioned for me to wait. She said something to Jonathan and handed him and two other children crayons and a sheet of paper.

What now? I thought, as she rustled through the door and took me aside. "I want to talk to you about Jonathan," she said.

I prepared myself for the worst. Nothing would have surprised me.

"Did you know Jonathan brought flowers to school today?" she asked.

I nodded, trying to keep the hurt in my eyes from showing. I glanced at my son busily coloring a picture. His wavy hair was too long and flopped just beneath his brow. He pushed it away with the back of his hand. His eyes burst with blue as he admired his handiwork.

"Let me tell you about yesterday," the teacher insisted. "See that little girl?"

I watched the rosy-cheeked child laugh and point to a colorful picture taped to the wall. I nodded.

"Well, yesterday she was almost hysterical. Her mother and father are going through a nasty divorce. Tish said she didn't want to live, she wished she could die. I watched that child bury her face in her hands and say loud enough for the class to hear, 'Nobody loves me.' I did all I could to console her but it only seemed to make matters worse."

"I thought you wanted to talk to me about Jonathan," I said.

"I do," she said, touching the sleeve of my blouse. "Your son came straight for Tish. I watched him hand her the flowers and whisper, 'I love you, Tish'."

I felt my heart swell with pride. "Thank you," I said, smiling and reaching for Jonathan's hand, "You've made my day."

Later that evening, I began pulling weeds from around my lopsided azalea bush. As I let my mind wander back to the love Jonathan showed the little girl, a verse from the Bible sprang to my mind: "And now these three remain: faith, hope, and love. But the greatest of these is love" (I Corinthians 13:13 NIV). My son knew what God said and put it into practice. But all day I had only thought of how angry I was. I dropped my head and whispered, "Forgive me, Lord."

I heard the familiar squeak of my husband's truck brakes as he pulled into the drive. I snapped a small limb bristling with hot pink azaleas off the bush. I felt the seed of love that God planted beginning to bloom once again in me.

My husband's eyes widened in surprise as I handed him the flowers. "I love you," I said.

—Nanette Thorsen-Snipes

My First Pair Of Roller Skates

As the youngest and only girl in a family of six children, I soon learned how each brother contributed to the income of the family. They accepted the responsibility of caring and sharing for each other as they went about their jobs and contributed to the family coffers each week.

When Joe turned twelve, he obtained a paper route. Proud of his work, Joe always knew who was sick, who had a new baby or a new litter of puppies. With his friendly manner he scattered cheerfulness like confetti along his paper route.

Each week he paid nine cents per paper for his week's supply and then collected twelve cents percustomer hoping no one had moved away and left an unpaid bill. He handed a dollar of his earnings to Mother before claiming any of the money for himself.

When Joe invited me to go with him on his paper route, I was thrilled and quickly learned which papers to throw on the porch and which ones to take to the door and ring the doorbell.

By carefully saving, he bought himself a pair of roller skates he had been eyeing in the window of Riddleman's Variety Store. Now he could deliver his papers twice as fast.

But the new speed eliminated the possibility of a short legged sister tagging along. He must have missed my company because he decided to teach me how to skate. We sat on the front porch as he adjusted the skates with the key to fit my shoes. Then he strapped them on and pulled me to my feet.

I wouldn't budge.

"Come on, Sis. Just put one foot in front of the other."

Each time I started to fall, he held on so I didn't hit the ground. We moved slowly to the end of the block. Sometimes he almost let loose of my hand. "See," he praised, "You're getting the hang of it."

We turned around and started back. "Now let's see you do it all by yourself." He shook his hand loose of my grip and gave me a slight shove. I skated almost to our porch before my skates rolled over a large crack in the sidewalk and I fell. We both laughed as I got up and tried again. I continued to practice my skating whenever Joe let me use his skates.

As spring afternoons grew longer and evenings warmer, skating became a popular sport around the neighborhood. While only the major streets were paved, all the other streets at least had sidewalks suitable for skating. However, sharing one pair of skates always left one of us as just an observer. Since Joe owned the skates, that usually was me.

One day I saw Mom and Joe whispering about something, but they stopped when they saw me. That evening Joe asked me to go with him on his paper route for the first time in a long, long time. Mother had a twinkle in her eye.

We proceeded on the paper route, Joe skating and I running hard to keep up. When one customer saw us, he chided Joe. "Don't you think you ought to let your sister skate awhile? Look at her short legs and your long ones."

My brother gave him a broad smile, "I'm going to let her skate all the way home."

At last we reached Riddleman's Store, the last stop on the route. All fifty papers had been delivered. Joe took off his skates before entering the store.

Mr. Riddleman smiled at us. "I see you brought your helper along today." Then he disappeared into the back room. I felt as if something special was about to happen.

He returned with a shoe box. My brother carefully counted out one dollar and seventy-five cents which he slid across the counter.

Stepping from behind the counter, Mr. Riddleman handed the heavy box to me. Everyone broke into big smiles as Joe lifted the lid. "Now Sis, you can skate all the way home."

Nestled in tissue paper were shiny new skates. He helped me put them on and adjusted them to fit my shoes. Then he took my hand and together we skated all the way home.

My brother gave me more than a pair of skates that day. He gave me memories to cherish and a heritage to treasure.

—Sarah Healton

ANYBODY HOME?

EVERY month before attending my Bible study at church, I would tell my three-year-old son, Chad, we were going to God's house. Each time we walked through the quiet sanctuary on our way to the nursery, Chad looked around in awe. One particular day, he stopped abruptly and asked "Mommy, if this is God's house, how come He's never home?"

—Karen Ketzler

Deferred Dreams

Dad sat with a far away mist in his eyes
Knowing his desires couldn't all come true
Then he looked at me with a smile that said
"My dreams are really for you."

He guided my path to the hillsides
Through orchards and somewhere beyond
Along the trail of mint leaves
Growing beside the backyard pond.

He encouraged my trip to the stars
As the notched wooden swing met the breeze
I clutched the ropes with my heart afire
Yearned for horizons beyond the trees.

We laughed up at ragged clouds
As Dad taught me to balance two wheels
I pushed off and climbed to other worlds
Released to all a young girl can feel.

To meet the needs of family
Dad gave his dreams away
Still he yearned and waited
For me to pick them up someday.

Today I leave laundry and dishes
Torn, though my pen flows free
And I hear Dad's voice bridge through time
Clearly saying, "Do it for me."

—Doris Hays Toppen

The Forgiving Formula

Several years ago my husband left the pastorate, and we moved from Rockford, Illinois, to St. Paul, Minnesota. I left behind a tremendous nest of prayer support, but I was confident I could find people in St. Paul to support my ministry in prayer. Soon after we moved, I was scheduled to speak at a prayer breakfast, and I found a few prayer chains to pray for me. When I got back, I called to thank the chairman for the prayer support. She said, "Oh, but we didn't pray." She went on to explain that someone in the church had stopped the prayer chain, because it was not their practice to pray for public speakers.

I was extremely hurt by this. The next week I went away with my husband and another couple to a mountain cabin. All week long I tried reading my Bible and praying, but I could not get through to God. I confessed my sins until I was blue in the face. Finally, Thursday morning at 5:30, I got up and went far from the cabin and threw myself on my face before God. I said, "Lord, say something. I don't care what you say, but say something."

I was beginning to panic, because I was teaching prayer seminars and yet God had not said a word to me all week. I started leafing through the Bible. When I got to II Corinthians 2:5, God stopped me. "If anyone has caused grief, he has not so much grieved me as he has grieved all of you."

That was my problem. I had been grieved, and amazingly God didn't disagree with me. When we are hurt by other Christians, we somehow feel that God sweeps it under the rug and says, "Don't worry about it." But he doesn't ignore it; he expects us to acknowledge that we have been grieved.

I was ready to get up from my knees and go make breakfast, thinking "Hallelujah, God agrees with me. I've been grieved." But God nudged me and said, "Don't stop—there is more in this chapter."

So I continued reading until I came to verse 7, "Now instead, you ought to forgive and comfort him so that he will not be overwhelmed by excessive sorrow."

I was supposed to forgive her. But how could I do that? She had made a fool of me. I had been the chairman of a prayer movement, prayer was my life, and when I had asked a simple prayer request, I had been slapped in the face, so to speak. It horrified me.

I waited on my knees a long time. I struggled with the Lord. Finally I said, "God, I can't do it on my own strength. You are going to have to help me."

And God did. His power, his grace, his ability to forgive came, and I forgave her. And as I forgave her, I paved the way for God to forgive me. In the Lord's Prayer, Jesus said, "Forgive us our debts as we also have forgiven our debtors" (Matthew 6:12). We are forgiven as we forgive.

But there was even more. God nudged me to read verse 8: "I urge you, therefore, to reaffirm your love for him." Since I didn't love that woman very much, I had to ask God for love. Again, I waited. The waiting was hard, but it was important. So often we ask God for something, and then we get right up and run away. So I waited until the love of God came.

I knew that not only did I have to love her in my heart, I had to show my love for her. Since I was on a mountain with no postal delivery or phone, I had to wait until we returned home and I met her in church.

The next Sunday morning the woman who had hurt me was sitting in the front of the church, and I was sitting in the back. During the service I prayed, "Lord, I do love her, and I want to affirm my love for her, but I'm not going to make a fool of myself." I kept trying to think how I could get out of it. Finally I made a bargain with the Lord that if she got to the back entry hall of the church before I got there, I would affirm my love for her. I thought I was safe, since I was a hundred feet closer to the hall.

But she got there first. People were watching us to see what I was going to do. They knew I went around teaching prayer seminars, and they wanted to know what I would do when I was hurt. I went up and put my arms around her and we settled it.

That was the hardest lesson in forgiveness I have ever learned, but forgiving that woman freed me to hear God again.

—Evelyn Christenson

Broken Pieces

I could hear the door of the china cabinet being opened and knew immediately that our three-year-old daughter had succumbed to temptation. Ever since learning to walk, she had been told repeatedly to "look, but don't touch." Yet her childish heart had been captivated by the sight of a ceramic hen that sat on the lowest shelf of the china cabinet. Underneath it in the "nest" were two white "eggs"—in reality a pair of salt and pepper shakers. The little red hen had been a unique wedding gift from old Aunt Susan, now gone home to be with the Lord, and I fully expected that one day I would pass on the treasured keepsake to our daughter.

At the moment, however, I was angry and impatient as I rushed into the dining room to retrieve it from her childish fingers. As I met her coming towards me, however, she was walking ever so carefully, trying her utmost to cradle the precious hen in her chubby fingers. "Look, Mommy, isn't it pretty?" She raised it up for me to admire, but as she did so, it slipped from her grasp and fell, shattering to pieces at our feet.

Expecting a stern rebuke, she stared up at me, wide-eyed and frightened, the tears brimming in her innocent blue eyes. My anger melted as I knelt down to console her. "It's all right, honey. You didn't mean to break it. It's just a dish. Come, help me sweep up the pieces."

Her sobs gradually subsided as she held the dust pan for me. Together we emptied the shards of broken glass into the garbage can and I gave her another reassuring hug as I gently closed the china cabinet door.

For several years thereafter I had trouble dismissing the incident from my mind. I kept seeing myself in the actions of our little girl—my fascination with things "off limit" to my Christian walk, my clumsy attempts to bring them to the Lord, hoping for His stamp of approval, the ongoing problem of priorities, the feelings of devastation when cherished hopes were dashed. After reading II Corinthians 4:7: "We have this treasure in earthen vessels," I sat down and summarized the truth as I saw it in the above poem. It was published in *Decision Magazine*.

Earthenware

So keen to try
I handle life with pride
until one day
it slips
between my hands
and crashes down
around me.
Shattered
I wait for God
to cry and shout
"I told you so!"
Instead
He stoops
to where I fall
and picking up
the broken parts
He says
"Don't cry.
It's only earthenware,
that's all."

Five years later I received a letter from a woman in Oklahoma. "Your poem," she wrote, "Blessed me so much at a very difficult time in my life. My husband's company folded and we lost our home, but not our love for God. I learned slowly to realize that everything we use in this world including the temple we live in is only earthenware. Your poem is on the wall in my bedroom. I think of it everyday. May God bless you always."

Her letter arrived the day after our daughter graduated from Bible School. She could not even recall dropping the treasured dish, but God had used a poem about the broken pieces to sustain the faith of a sister in Christ.

It had taken over seventeen years, but in the economy of God, I had been shown the true value of the treasured keepsake.

—Alma Barkman

A Grandmother

A Grandmother is a lady who no longer has young children. She loves other people's children. A grandmother doesn't do anything much but sit there. They always have plenty of food when you come to lunch or dinner. They are so old they shouldn't play hard or run. It is enough for them if they drive with us to the market. If they take us for walks they slow down past pretty things like leaves and caterpillars. We should never say to them, "hurry up."

Usually they are fat, but sometimes they are thin. They are never too fat to be able to tie our shoes. They wear glasses and funny underwear. They can take their teeth and gums out. They don't have to be smart, only smart enough to answer questions like, "Why do dogs hate cats?" and "How come God is not married?" When they read to us they don't skip pages or even mind if it is the same story over and over again. Everybody should have one—especially if you don't have a T.V. because grandmothers are sometimes the only grownups who have time for us.

We should always be thankful for our grandmothers.

—**Unknown**

Hugging

Hugging is healthy . . .

It helps the body's immune system
It keeps you healthier
It cures depression
It reduces stress
It induces sleep
It's invigorating and rejuvenating
It has no unpleasant side effects

Hugging is nothing less than a miracle drug . . .

All natural; organic
Naturally sweet
100% wholesome
No pesticides
No preservatives
No artificial ingredients

Hugging is practically perfect: there are no movable parts, no batteries to wear out, no periodic checkups, low energy consumption, high energy yield, inflation-proof, non-fattening, no monthly payments, no insurance requirements, theft-proof, non-taxable, non-polluting, and of course, fully returnable.

—Unknown

9

Marriage

For this cause a man shall leave his father and his mother, and shall cleave to his wife; and they shall become one flesh.

Genesis 2:24

He's No Mind Reader

As a newlywed, I used to think, "If Steve really loved me he could read my mind." One day I finally realized how ridiculous I was being. No human being can read someone else's mind. I was expecting Steve to be God. From then on I would say to Steve, "Tell me you think I'm beautiful, I'm waiting. Tell me you think I'm smart. Tell me you love me." Though I would say it jokingly, I wanted him to understand what I needed from him emotionally and with time he did.

—**Annie Chapman**

Touch

It is when I am supposed to be sleeping that I feel closest to him. Days of hard, outdoor labor will bed him before me, especially in winter's deep freeze. He needs his sleep, but when I crawl under the covers made so hot by his body, I have to reach for him—if only to touch my fingertips to his arm, his back, his shoulder. My touch connects us, and I am real.

He is a light sleeper, though not as light as I. As I disturb the blankets, he sighs and turns, moving away, his back toward me, concerned only with slumber. I chide myself for being hurt somewhat. But a hand on his back, on the smooth of his head, which he loathes and I adore, brings him toward me like a child into my lap, and we curl up like spoons. Almost the same length, we are a perfect fit, and I am whole again.

Each night this dance, joined by love, split by a heat too visceral to comprehend. Joined again, minimal surfaces touching: forehead to forehead, my hand in his. Higher on the pillow, his head beneath mine, something maternal yearning. Again, the heat. Again, this dance.

In the morning I find him reaching for me, and I am awed once again that we love this much.

—**Debora Allen**

View From An Empty Nest

Twenty years ago when I first heard the term "empty nest" it sounded like a very pleasant position to be in. Just think, waking up in the morning fully rested instead of having your eyes pried open by tiny fingers.

In an empty nest, I could wear clothes without spit-up stains, finish sentences when speaking to my husband, and carry a purse without squeak toys, pacifiers, or cookie crumbs laying in wait inside.

Oh, the beauty of dinnertime without spilled milk, a house without the background sounds of crying and being able to sleep through an entire night. I could push a shopping cart that was filled with groceries instead of children!

Recently, when I reached that sought-after goal, I felt very smug. No "empty nest syndrome" for me. That was mere psychological gibberish. I adjusted the very first week with no problems at all.

However, the second week I became aware that a subtle stillness had fallen over our house. I noticed the telephone had ceased ringing and laughter no longer echoed from the back of the house.

I tried not to look into the three empty bedrooms as I passed by them. Even though the beds were all neatly made, the rooms lacked character. The one-eyed teddy bear was missing from his favorite spot on the floor. School books, papers, and cans of hair spray had all disappeared. The closet doors covered vacant areas that at one time had been stuffed beyond their limits.

Up close, the empty nest no longer looked quite as attractive. This was partly because the ensuing years had automatically solved many of the distasteful parts of motherhood. For some time now, no one had been spitting up on me or crying to be fed in the middle of the night. No one had to be bathed, or dressed, or have their shoes tied ten times a day. Just when the children became pleasant company, they moved out. Is there no justice?

When I finally crept out of my depression to take a peek around me, I noticed my dear husband, looking almost the same as he had when I had fallen wildly in love with him. Except for a bit of wear and tear, the years have been good to him. I fondly looked at the gray hairs at his temple, knowing exactly where they had come from. But I caught myself grinning when I realized that the creases on his face are smile lines, not worry wrinkles. Yes, we have had our share of fun.

As I sat gazing at him, I realized my nest was not empty after all. It still held the one special person God had given me to share my life with. In the quiet of the empty nest it would be easier for us to find each other. As I looked at him I wondered if maybe, just maybe, we could rekindle the sparks we had originally ignited. And then, as if to answer my unspoken question, he looked up at me and winked.

—June Cerza Kolf

Learning To Trust

Several years ago, I turned my internal battle on my husband, Bill, and began to fight him for my every goal. In turn, he began to battle me for time as well. Overall, our marriage was good, often passionate, but a wall was rising between us. We struggled to pinpoint its cause through numerous discussion sessions. Each of us felt this wall growing brick by brick. But the recurring tension between us made it obvious we still hadn't found the tool to knock it down.

One night, right in the middle of a heated discussion, we both looked at each other and said, "We have to pray—now!" We fell to our knees. Neither one of us wanted to talk to God or each other, but we did it anyway. We held hands, not because we wanted to but because we knew we had to join hands as a symbol of good will, just as boxers touch gloves at the end of a fight. As we each poured out the ugliness and frustration that was locked inside, we began to see the pattern that had been battering our marriage—*we didn't trust one another!*

We had always prided ourselves on the amount of trust we had in our marriage. I knew Bill was on my side; he was my biggest fan. Bill had often bragged about how much he had accomplished personally and professionally because I had been such a cheerleader for him. It shocked us that the subtle battle in our own minds to "have it all" had stripped us of the ability to believe that the other wanted the best for *both* of us. We threw up the white flags and began to talk again, this time in calm conversation. Together we have been prying individual bricks out of the wall that had been keeping us apart.

Over a period of several days, Bill and I realized that we needed to step back and take a good, hard look at where we were and where we wanted to be. As we were driving home from a ministry obligation, Bill pulled the car to the side of the road. The lights of the city lay quiet and calm ahead of us, a stark contrast to the frothing discontentment rising in each of our hearts.

"Pam, I love you—I want you to know that right from the start. I can't keep going like this."

"Me either," I said as tears welled up in my eyes. "We need a break. I can't even see things clearly anymore. Sometimes I battle for things that I know shouldn't be that important to me."

"And I take all your obligations and goals as a personal insult—like you don't want to spend time with me."

"Oh, I love spending time with you. A lot of what I do is for you—or at least I thought it was."

"Bill, we need to get away, together, and really deal with this." And we began to arrange for three days on our own in a quiet place where nobody knows us. Those days proved wonderfully significant and healing.

During the next few days after we came home, we each shopped for a small token or symbol of the dream that we thought was most precious to our spouse.

I opened the large flat box Bill handed me. I found a beautiful briefcase. Inside the case were several small packages. A small card on the first one read, "I believe in you." Inside was a gift certificate for me to order business cards for the home-based business I wanted to start when the semester ended.

The next gift was slightly larger and it had a note that read, "I believe in us." Inside was a daytime organizer with red hearts marking "Date with Bill" once every week for the first month. A specially marked weekend was noted with the message "See package three." Package three was a brochure for a place I had said I'd love to go "next time we get away." One tiny package remained—a picture of Bill and the boys with a card that read, "Thanks for all the time you spend making us a family."

I handed Bill his gifts. There were five different colored envelopes, each containing a card. The first card contained the recipe for Bill's favorite meal and a note that said, "My heart has been away from home but I want to sit at our candlelit table and share this with you. It's in the freezer. You pick the day and time."

Card two contained a few certificates to a driving range. "You gave up golf to spend more time with the boys and me. We want to come watch you practice."

Card three was a handmade coupon for an evening of Monday night football without distractions.

Card four was attached to a box containing a tie and a Post-it note that said, "For those power lunches."

The last card contained a poem describing our time away on the getaway, including references to how much I enjoyed intimacy with Bill.

I said quietly, "Thanks Bill. Thanks for listening and believing in me. I love you."

Bill leaned across, lightly kissed me and whispered, "Thanks, Angel. I really did miss you. You're the best."

Later that evening, as we walked hand in hand toward our bedroom, I said, "Thanks for being patient with me through all this stress."

Bill smiled and nodded, "Pam, thanks for your patient love toward me."

We have discovered that "love does not consist in gazing at each other but in looking together in the same direction." (Antoine de Saint-Exupery)

—**Pam Farrel**

*The Nurse From Home Improvement

Do any of us really think that the vow, "in sickness and in health" will have to be tested the first six months of marriage? We certainly didn't. When I found a lump during my monthly breast self-examination, I was overwhelmed.

Before long, I had been squished, prodded and x-rayed until I glowed. Still, after all this, we were informed that they still couldn't accurately diagnose the lump. Surgery to remove only the lump and biopsy it was the last and most definitive method. In the midst of my tears, a trembling lip, and asking "Why me?" My husband, Lynn, in typical fix-it-male fashion, said, "Let's get that thing out of there!" Together we both prayed and cried.

After my surgery, the biggest challenge turned out not to be waiting for the pathology reports. It was feeling clean and comfortable with only sponge baths. I found myself getting crankier and more frustrated, taking it out on the person nearest and dearest to me. Lynn is a patient, loving and godly man. However, in his frustration, he blurted out, "What can I *do*? Give me something I can *do* for you!"

I begged, "Please figure out a way I can take a hot shower and wash my hair, while insuring the surgical dressing will stay dry."

Lynn set out on his task. His purpose had been defined and his assignment determined. Upon returning with all sorts of tools, he instructed me to let him put his plan into action. A half hour later he pronounced his masterpiece watertight.

As I passed by the bathroom mirror on the way to nirvana called my shower, I glanced at myself. First, curiosity, "What the . . ?" Then, I looked closer to what he had done. My shoulders started to shake uncontrollably and we both burst out laughing. He had wrapped my B-cup in gauze until I looked like Dolly Parton. This whole unit was put in a heavy-duty zip-lock plastic bag and then sealed around the edges with bright blue, two-inch tape used to mask the windows when we painted the house.

This was the turning point in my dread over the possible outcome of the biopsy. I knew that we could face anything together with God right beside us. And, that I was one blessed woman the day the Lord joined us and we each said, "I do." Not only does God provide a method to lighten us up by encouraging us to give up our concerns to Him, He provides "lightening up" by giving us a way to laugh and release some of the burden immediately.

—Connie Merritt

A Kiss From Jesus

After lunch one day, my two-and-a-half-year-old daughter, Sophie, and I walked to the playground in our mobile home park. Sophie, eager to play, climbed up the ladder to the top of the slide. She paused, looked intently at me and proclaimed, "Mommy, Jesus loves you."

"Well, thank you for telling me Sophie," I smiled.

Instead of sliding down as she always did, she suddenly climbed back down the ladder and ran over to me.

"Mommy," she said, with eyes that pierced mine. "Jesus *really* loves you."

Before I could respond, Sophie was hugging me with such strength and purpose that I was speechless. And then she kissed me not once, but several times on my mouth.

"Sophie," I sighed, "What are you doing?" She had never kissed me on the mouth before, only on the cheek.

Again Sophie looked into my eyes. "Jesus *really* loves you and so do I, Mom."

I giggled out of embarrassment and giddiness.

"Well, I love you too, Sophie, and so does Jesus."

After I hugged her, she climbed back up onto the slide and slid down. She resumed her play as though nothing had happened.

I sat watching Sophie play and knew her hugs and kisses expressed more than her love for me. It really felt like Jesus was hugging me and kissing me through my daughter. Sophie had never expressed affection like that before. It wasn't until later that night that I understood why God had spoken to me so directly.

That evening, my husband, Craig, Sophie and I had a nice dinner, then spent some family time. After that Sohpie was put bed. Then Craig and I began discussing an issue until it escalated into a heated argument. With a knot swelling in my throat and hot tears welling up in my eyes, I escaped to our bedroom. I heard Craig turn on the television. I buried my face in our bedspread and wept bitterly. "Oh God, why doesn't Craig understand? It hurts so much when he doesn't hear me."

As my tears subsided, I remembered Sophie's words. "Jesus *really* loves you, Mommy!" Her strong hug and kisses embraced me again—as if Jesus were hugging and kissing me.

Fresh tears fell but these were mixed with joy and awe.

"You knew . . ." I whispered, "You knew, Jesus, that I would need to know tonight how much You love me."

Later, Craig went straight to sleep—too exhausted to talk. As I listened to him breathing deeply beside me, I thanked God for His love and care for me. He knew that under normal circumstances I could never sleep without resolving our argument. He also knew that in the morning we would be reconciled and our marriage would be stronger.

Rather than harboring anger, the memory of Jesus' hugs and kisses expressed to me through Sophie filled my heart.

"Yes, Jesus. You *really* do love me. And I love you too."

—Deborah Sillas Nell

Be My Friend

Fred and I have been married for more than forty years. We travel everywhere together. We're with one another around the clock, and we actually have fun. This hasn't always been the case.

Sixteen years into our marriage, we were both discouraged. In today's world we would have probably divorced, but we had a sense of commitment that kept us together. Neither Fred nor I had ever taken the time to develop listening skills or understand each other's unique personality. So, when we endured the excruciating loss of two brain-damaged sons, these weak spots nearly caused our marriage to give out.

There were no books, tapes, or seminars on grief or marriage at the time and, because neither of us was a good listener, we were unable to tend to the other's grief, much less address any of the ongoing issues in our marriage. Privately, we each resolved to stay married for the sake of our two daughters. The reality was that neither Fred nor I had bonded with each other emotionally, so we grew further and further apart as we tried to cope with the many difficult issues that faced us as parents of children with severe disabilities.

Whenever I tried to discuss my feelings about the dilemmas we faced, Fred would offer point-by-point solutions to each problem. He gave me quick answers to everything, but I didn't want answers. What I wanted was someone to listen to me without judging me or making me feel stupid. I wondered, "Is it too much to ask him to listen to me and take my feelings seriously?" Fred couldn't understand why anyone would want to waste time discussing a problem without coming up with an immediate solution. I, in turn, viewed his answers as a lack of compassion and empathy—a sign that he didn't care about me or what I was feeling.

One day I asked Fred, "Wouldn't you rather be my friend then my having to talk to six other women about a problem I'm having?"

"Of course I want to be your friend, Fred replied.

"I like my friends a lot better than you because they listen. They don't give me answers," I said.

My comment stopped Fred in his tracks. He finally understood that his answers, rather than solving my problems, only forced me to go to other people for emotional intimacy. He realized then that maybe he had better stop giving me advice and start listening.

—Florence Littauer

A Wealthy Woman

A wealthy woman who was traveling overseas saw a bracelet that she thought was irresistible so she sent her husband this cable:

Have found wonderful bracelet. Price $75,000. May I buy it?

Her husband promptly wired back this response:

No, price too high.

But the cable operator omitted the comma so the woman received this message:

No price too high.

Elated, she purchased the bracelet. Needless to say, when she returned home her husband was dismayed.

It was just a little thing—a comma—but what a difference it made!

—Unknown

DOUBLE IDENTITY

LAST summer, I taught a vacation Bible school class on Judas' betrayal of Jesus. After the lesson, I went over the review questions and asked, "Who betrayed Jesus for 30 pieces of silver!" Without hesitating, my seven-year old son, Kenny, replied, "I know it was 'Judas the scariest'!"

—Karen Weaver

10

Mothering

He makes the barren woman abide in the house as a joyful mother of children. Praise the Lord!

Psalm 113:9

The Point Is—Missing

As the parent of a small, trusting child in this big, scary world, I knew the time had come to warn my son of strangers. So one afternoon, I took him by the hand, sat beside him on the porch steps and began.

"You know, Joshua, not everyone is lucky enough to have their own child. Sometimes people without children want them so badly, they steal somebody else's child."

His eyes were intent on me. I was getting through.

"If a stranger offers you candy or toys or asks you to get into their car," I continued, "You scream as loud as you can and run home even faster. Because we don't want anyone to steal you."

I paused, allowing the words to sink in. Then, looking into big, saucer eyes, I asked, "Can you tell me what you learned from our talk today?"

He sat still, chin in hand, and pondered the question. After a very long silence, he answered. "I'm never EVER gonna' steal anybody else's kid."

—**Mary Bahr Fritts**

Moochie Letters

"Sure wish I'd get a letter." The disappointed voice of six-year-old Julie could barely be heard above the squeals of delight of the other young campers who stood around reading their mail.

Linda heard the plaintive remark made by her daughter as she stood with her group of campers at mail call. All the other girls in Julie's group received one or more letters, but not a single one arrived for Julie.

Letters from Julie's father addressed to Mrs. Linda Wagner arrived and were filled with grown up news. Linda was a counselor with an older group and always shared her letters with Julie as soon as she had a chance, but that wasn't the same as receiving one of her very own.

Today Linda saw her daughter, a dejected little girl, walk away from the group and back to her cot. She picked up her favorite book and began to read.

Linda knew her daughter used this method to deal with disappointments. She joined Julie and said, "I know you're disappointed you haven't gotten any letters yet. Your daddy is very busy going to school, along with his job. I'm here at camp with you so I can't write to you. Is there someone you could write to who would write back?"

Julie frowned. "All my friends have gone away for the summer. And I don't have a grandmother like the other girls. I wish Daddy would write me a letter."

"Daddy did put a note in my letter for you. He said he and your dog, Moochie, missed us."

"I wish Moochie could write me a letter." Longing filled Julie's voice.

This gave Julie's mother an idea. That night when all the campers were settled, Linda wrote her nightly letters to her husband and her son at the boy's camp on the other side of the lake. As soon as she finished, she printed a one page letter to Julie. It read:

Dear Julie,

Your daddy is very busy, so he asked me to write to you. Today, we went to the store. He bought ten TV dinners for himself and a box of dog biscuits for me. I watched him mow the lawn. I sit at his feet while he studies. The house is very quiet. I miss you and your brother very much.

Love,

Moochie.

The next day at mail call, a big smile crossed Julie's face when she heard her name called. Several girls in her group gathered around as she read her letter again and again.

"Who's your letter from?" Lisa asked.

"Moochie." Julie announced proudly.

"Who's Moochie?"

"She's our black cocker spaniel."

"Did she really write you this letter?" Lisa questioned.

Julie held up the envelope with the canceled stamp. "See, Here's the envelope. It came in the mail."

Each day after that, a letter arrived for Julie from Moochie. The girls in her group loved hearing from Moochie. They loved the dog's funny adventures.

"Julie's dog sure is smart," Lisa said to Debbie.

"Do you think her dog really writes those letters?" asked Vicky. "I bet her dad writes them."

"No, he doesn't," Debbie replied. "I've seen her dad's handwriting. He couldn't print neatly like that."

Soon packages filled with cookies began to arrive during mail call. All the campers crowded around the lucky recipient and shared the treats.

The same afternoon Linda drove to a nearby village and went to the bakery shop. The baker packed two nice boxes of cookies for her. One box she mailed to her son at his camp. The other box she mailed to Julie.

The next day a box arrived at camp for Julie. All her friends gathered around as she opened the box.

"Who's the box from?" Debbie tried to peep into the box.

Julie quickly read the card and held it high for all to see. "It's from Moochie."

Debbie's eyes grew big, "Did Moochie bake them?"

"Of course not!" Julie looked at her gullible friend. "She bought them at the bakery."

The following summer when Julie went to camp and her mother stayed home. As she kissed her mother good-bye before climbing on the camp bus, Julie whispered, "Mother, send me Moochie letters."

—Sarah Healton

I Used To . . .

I used to stretch my muscles frequently with exercise
and pride myself for being fit and careful with my size.

I used to wonder how to fill the hours at weeks end,
Running about or hanging out then sleeping in past ten!

I used to dream of growing wise and earning more degrees,
Adding to my name the honor of a Ph.D.

I used to long for status from the things I'd say and do . . .
Impressing those around me just because of what I knew.

But now my goals have changed a bit, for as a mom I'll be . . .
playing ball and riding bikes and dressing up for tea.

For now my muscle tone is shot, my skin sags here and there . . .
and where bikini lines once were stretch marks boldly glare.

So much for meals I had in peace, and time I had to spare,
Farewell to outings on my own and days without a care.

For now I dine in family style, with noodles here and there,
embracing sticky fingers as we thank the Lord in prayer.

So much for wisdom and degrees, of lofty goals for fame . . .
To being wise in others eyes and status by my name.

For now such wisdom would not help to solve the daily woes,
of broken dolls, and missing balls, of scrapes to knees and toes.

I'm not sure how it would have been if they weren't in my life . . .
Oh sure I'd have free time again and probably much less strife.

But somehow all I used to do just simply can't compare . . .
To sharing in their journeys through each hope and each despair.

So thank you Lord for helping me give up some hopes and dreams . . .
In order that I know first-hand what fullness really means!

—Patty Stump

Tribute

How often in my own life did my parents pray me through the obstacles that could have stymied my development! And it has been prayer that gave Bill and me the hope and confidence that God would see our children through.

In my experience it has often been the kids themselves who lifted and encouraged me as a parent. A letter Benjy gave me for my birthday when he was sixteen kept me from "throwing in the towel" on some of my dreams. Suzanne insisting, when she was fourteen, that Bill and I continue singing even though it was hard for them to have us gone a lot, kept me from quitting a ministry God has been able to use. And this poem from Amy when she was away at college, let me know that maybe, just maybe, we had done something right.

Minus One

I think of you, sitting by the fire,
Coffee mug beside you,
Letter spread out on your lap.
The dogs lie quietly at your feet,
Stretched out in private dreams.
I smell hot apple cider,
And vegetable soup simmering on the stove,
The clock is ticking on the mantle,
And the world is silent on the November afternoon;
The gray mist outside is held at bay
By our warm walls—
And I am not there to see you.
But I know—
And when I close my eyes,
And feel you missing me, as I miss you,
Home is not so very far away.

—Gloria Gaither & Amy Gaither, age 18

Things Eternal

"Remember what's important," I kept chanting under my breath as I surveyed the damage. My son stood holding his hand, grimacing in pain and looking at me with his big brown eyes beseeching me to please understand.

He had decided that he wanted to make a big crayon, so he had peeled a dozen or so broken ones, put them in a pan, and stuck it in the oven. When he asked permission to do this, I took a deep breath. Here I was in the middle of making dinner, two of my children had friends over, and my husband had just called to say he was going to be late. "Okay, go ahead," I said, and turned back to the pizza dough. A short time later I heard a cry and a crash.

When I turned around, there he was, squeezing his hand. And there was the melted crayon splattered all over the top of my new kitchen counter, staining it. Anger built inside me. In recent weeks, several of my precious possessions had been broken: a tortoise shell comb inherited from my great-grandmother and an antique spice jar from Japan that my mom gave me before she died. Even our new kitchen floor had several gouges in it already. Couldn't *anything* stay nice in this house?

And hadn't this been a trying enough day: listening to my children's whining, changing diapers, seemingly endless piles of laundry and dirty dishes? This mess was it. The last straw!

As my mouth opened to deliver hot words of rebuke, I suddenly thought of something my husband had asked me recently. "Honey," he asked me, "What will be important ten years from now?"

I looked at my precious child. The one who gave me hugs and told me that I was the "bestest examundo mom in the whole world." The boy who drew a picture that said "I love my mom" and hung it on the front door to greet me. The one I found snuggled up with his little brothers on the living room sofa, reading aloud from their favorite story book.

I looked at him grasping his hand, burned from impulsively grabbing a hot pan. I saw tears welling in his beautiful brown eyes, partly because he hurt, partly because he felt terrible about what had happened. *What will be important in ten years?* A stain on the counter? Better that than a stain on my child's heart. Better that I give him the memory of a mom hugging him when he hurt instead of yelling because he was clumsy.

So, I swallowed hard, bent down and said, "That's okay, honey. It was just an accident. Let's put some ice on your finger."

When the pizza was done, and the children were eating, I stood in the kitchen slowly scraping multicolored globs of crayon. I felt a small hand slip into mine and a quiet voice say "I'm really sorry, mom. Thanks for not getting mad." I was thankful, too.

And guess what? There's no stain left. Not on my counter. And not on my child's heart.

—Elaine Munyan

Love Letters To My Unborn Child

I was twenty-two-years old, and had been married for only one year. We were young and in love, and working hard to build a happy life together as a couple. The wonderful news that we were expecting a baby in seven months was both exciting and scary. In my youthful enthusiasm I came up with the idea of writing "love letters" to our baby to express my feelings of expectancy and joy. Little did I know just how valuable those "love letters" would be in years to come.

August, 1971: Oh my darling baby, can you feel the love I have for you while you are so small and living in the quiet world inside my body? Some day you too may know the changes a woman feels when she is pregnant. A new life . . . a pure soul . . . so beautiful and untouched. How can I make life wonderful for you? Your daddy and I want the world to be perfect for you. No hate, no wars, no pollution. I can't wait to hold you in my arms! I love you and daddy loves you too; but he can't feel you yet.

September, 1971: I can tell you are growing. I've been taking my vitamins and eating healthy foods for you. Thank goodness my morning sickness is gone. I think about you all the time. Our love will try to guide you; to help you on the road of life which you eventually must walk alone.

October, 1971: Oh, these melancholy moods. I cry so often over so little. Sometimes I feel very alone, and then I remember you are growing inside of me. I feel stirring now, a tumbling, turning and pushing. It's never the same. Your movements always bring me so much joy! I love you, my baby.

November, 1971: I am feeling much better now that my fatigue and nausea have passed. I feel your movements often now. Constant punching and kicking. Last week daddy and I were thrilled to hear your loud, strong heartbeat at the doctor's office. We love you so.

February 2, 1972, at 11:06 p.m., our baby girl Sasha was finally born. It was a long, hard labor, and your daddy helped me to relax and stay as calm as possible. We are so happy to see you, to hold you, and to greet your pretty face. Welcome!

Many years have passed since those "love letters" were written to my daughter. Time passed quickly. My husband and I jokingly said that we put our five-year-old daughter to bed one night, and she woke up a teen-ager the next morning.

Those few years of adolescence and rebellion were not easy. There were times my beautiful, yet angry teen-ager would dig her feet into the ground and yell out to me, "I hate you! You never loved me! You don't care about me or want me to be happy!" Her harsh words cut at my heart like a razor-edged knife, and I would privately weep wondering what I could have done wrong.

During one of my daughter's angry outbursts I suddenly remembered the little box of "love letters" I'd written to her during my pregnancy. Later that day, I found them and quietly placed them on her bed hoping she would read them. A few days later she appeared before me with tears in her eyes and a contrite tender attitude on her face.

She shared that she had no idea just how much I truly loved her even before she was born. "How could you love me without knowing what I looked like, or if I would be deformed or ugly? You loved me unconditionally!"

That very precious moment between us became a bond of unity that still exists today. Somehow those dusty old "love letters" meant so much to her and they amazingly melted away the anger and rebellion she had been feeling.

No one can resist words of unconditional love!

—Judith Hayes

Speaking With Kindness To My Children

"Would you please hand me the book that fell on the floor?" asked a woman's pleasant voice behind me. I turned around from where I stood in the checkout line at our local library to see if she was talking to me. She wasn't. She had directed her request to her three-year-old son.

This woman's gentle tone of voice caught me by surprise. Here she stood, talking to her young child as politely as if she talked with the librarian. I looked at my own two children and wondered if my voice sounded as kind as hers did when I talked with them.

Over the next several days, I listened to myself when I talked to my boys. I realized that I didn't talk very nicely to them. My tone of voice seemed to lack the respect and kindness that I used when I talked with other adults. Sometimes I sounded more commanding than was necessary. Other times I realized I sounded sarcastic and belittling.

I had always planned to raise my children to be examples of Jesus' love. I suddenly realized that I needed to be a better example myself of how to demonstrate His love towards others by simply talking nicer to my boys.

I began to read books about communication. It took a conscious effort to fight my natural impulses, but I began to use the skills I learned. Instead of yelling at the boys about a problem that developed, I calmly talked to them. I tried to show them how to be nice to each other by being a better example myself.

Years later, my husband and I walked into our child's first grade classroom for a parent conference. His teacher greeted us and said, "I think your son is the most polite student I've ever had." Her words filled me with thankfulness for the way God opened my ears to hear the kindness in that woman's voice at the library so long ago.

—**Nancy I. Sanders**

A Real Person

Thoughts swirled in my mind like the batter-covered beaters in the mixing bowl before me. Manuscript ideas vied for attention, as did my preschool-aged daughter shouting above the mixer's noise, the ringing telephone, the microwave timer, and my husband's questions about another check I forgot to enter.

Like pinging beebees at arcade ducks, I took care of each need in order. The cake went into the oven. My daughter received permission to water paint. The phone solicitor got three firm no's before a firmer "click" in his ear. The softened butter for frosting emerged from the microwave. My husband got an exact figure for the checkbook register.

Now, it was time for me.

I snuck upstairs to my writing office to steal a few quiet moments. Inspiration had been bubbling in me like rich spaghetti sauce in a pressure cooker. I wanted to jot down the meaty phrases and spicy metaphors before they wafted out the steam valve. My fingers flew over the keyboard, racing to keep pace with the words and phrases. And then . . .

"Mommy?"

I kept typing. *Just let me get this down . . . .*

"Mommy? . . . . . . Mommy? . . . . . . Mom? . . . MOM!"

"WHAT!" I wheeled to face my daughter, standing before me in her painting smock. "Why, for just five minutes," I snapped, "Can't I be a real person?"

"But you can't be a real person when your little child needs you," she replied in innocent wisdom.

Ouch.

I took Elizabeth's paint-stained hands in mine and pulled her close. She chattered about her paintings of castles and dinosaurs from the past, but my thoughts went to the future. When I'm an empty-nester looking back, what will I see?

With enough drive and determination, this writing career could pay off big. I pictured glistening copies of my books fanned over a designer table. A leather-topped executive desk cluttered with publishing contracts and invitations to speak. And my adult children not returning my calls.

With enough patience and love, this parenting thing could pay off, too. I imagined snapshots and art work from the grandkids covering my refrigerator. The wall calendar marked with birthdays, school programs, and expected visits. And my magnum opus still in a ragged file-folder.

Which scenario would I choose if I had the power? Honestly, I want the good aspects of both. With enough creativity and time, perhaps it will happen. But one thing is certain: I've never heard a woman express regret over spending too much time with her family. Besides, being a "real" person means staying accessible to people—even little people with endless little needs.

". . . and then the princess put on her pink dress and pink shoes with the sparkles all over them. What do you think, Mommy?"

Cupping Elizabeth's round face in my hand, her eyes filled with eagerness, I spoke straight from my heart.

"I think we should paint a picture of that . . . together."

—**Debi Stack**

Happy Father's Day, Mom!

We know you're not really our dad, Mom, but in so many ways you are. We just wanted to say thanks for all the "dad things" you've done for us but they don't make Father's Day cards for single moms.

Thanks for teaching us that the screwdriver with that criss-cross point is called a Phillips; and for showing us that the handle also doubles well as a hammer.

Thanks for teaching us to clean up our rooms because women just aren't interested in slobby bachelors; not even knowing what a bachelor was at the time!

Thanks for allowing the belching contests we boys needed to display our fledging manhood. Oh, and thanks for letting us win sometimes.

Thanks for letting us flirt with girls and test our masculinity without feeling jealous or threatened, (you know you were always #1 Mom); and thanks for defending us when their boyfriends came around.

Thanks for taking in stride all our broken bones, cuts, scrapes, and emergencies; without fainting or throwing up.

Thanks for teaching us about the birds and the bees when nobody else wanted to; and ignoring the looks we gave you for weeks after.

Thanks for teaching us how to pump gas and check the oil; and thanks for letting us know in your subtle way, Mom, that cars work best when the man takes care of these things.

Thanks for teaching us how to read a map like a man, and how to fold it back up like a woman.

And when the money was tight, thanks for showing us that a little bit of imagination stretches a lot farther than a dollar.

Thanks for showing us that real men had better eat quiche!

And thanks, Mom, for teaching us to trust in Jesus; the One from whom all blessings flow.

Thanks for being a good example of being a provider, and for preparing us to be good husbands and fathers from a woman's perspective. We learned how to be men from you, Mom, by your example of what a woman wants a man to be.

And Mom, in spite of what happened to you, thanks for teaching us that marriage is good, and that a Father is to be honored.

We honor you, Mom.

Happy Father's Day.

—Jeri Chrysong

WHOSE HOUSE?

MY family is close friends with another family who faithfully attends church. Often we spend Sunday afternoons together relaxing at our house. Recently, when I phoned our friends, their four-year-old daughter, Alicia, answered and politely asked who was calling. To tease her, I said kiddingly, "Alicia, you come to my house almost every Sunday and you don't know who I am?" In a reverential voice she replied breathlessly, "Jesus?"

—Stacey Penalva

Mommy Resolves . . .

"Whatcha doing, Mommy?" my youngest asks, as I hover over a yellow tablet, while chewing on my eraser, working on my New Year resolutions.

"Trying to shove a nickel into a dime meter," I answer. Jeremy is standing beside me with his "I actually used soap" grin that shines on his fat little cheeks.

"Maybe your meter will take a penny," Jeremy answers.

As I look into blue, blue eyes, I wonder how he came to be so wise. Wise enough to realize that maybe I'm trying to squeeze in four cents too many. But then he does see the daily battles Bill and I wage in the war to become Superdad and Supermom.

"Why don't you help me write my New Year's resolutions," I ask, "After you change your soggy towel for some pajamas?"

"Okay," he answers, drying himself on the run, allowing me a glimpse of the other "cheek" part of that perfect little body. Which reminds me to write that same old "top of the list" resolution: "I will exercise regularly." That's the one that comes to mind every year with the speed of light, surpassed only by the warp speed with which I'm able to forget.

"What's a *nooyersolution?*" he asks, plopping himself down at the kitchen table with his Red Chief tablet, soggy pajamas and uncombed hair reaching out like a window-box fern.

"It's something I promise to do at the beginning of each New Year . . . something that'll make me a better . . . mother."

"And me a better father," my husband adds as he searches the kitchen for the stash of chocolate cookies he told me to hide from him. Needless to say, Bill tops his list with that same exercise resolution.

As I observe the speed with which our son is already writing, I'm forced to wonder how much better he thinks I should be.

"Read them to me," he hands me his list.

"I'd rather listen to you read." I chicken out as I see words I might mispronounce like dux, klim, and funi.

"Can I listen, too?" Bill sits down conspicuously with milk and *no* cookies. Does he want Jeremy's suggestions, too? Does he want to see how far I fall short of our child's expectations? Or does he just want to know where I hid the chocolate cookies?

Jeremy begins, reading with the language Mark Twain describes best: "You can't depend upon your eyes if your imagination is out of focus." Jeremy's eyes are most definitely 20/20.

Mommy's List

Not to sniff funny like you do when we pick up my brother from basketball practice.
Don't stir stuff on the stove when I'm reading to ya.
Fasten your own seat belt.
Don't say "careful" so loud when I climb out on the rocks to feed the ducks on the lake.
Believe me when I say I don't need a bath.
Stop telling me about vitamins when I pack my lunch box by myself.
Not to laugh loud after I have to go to bed so you don't wake me up.
To yell nice things at the driver in front of our car.

"It's your bedtime, sweetie." I cuddle my wise man, hoping he doesn't see my tears of thanks, that this one is young enough still to smell the roses.

As he runs down the hallway toward his bedroom, Bill and I both erase that meaningless top of the list resolution. And we scribble frantically all the really important ideas our little one has brought to mind.

". . . And one for you, Dad," he yells on his way downstairs.

"I'm listening, son."

"Share the chocolate cookies with me that Mom always hides in the garage."

I swear Bill had tears in his eyes, too, as he rushed out the back door.

—Mary Bahr Fritts

The Eye Of The Beholder

I watched my four-year-old as he stood on the kitchen chair he'd dragged close to the wall. He stared intensely at the painting hanging there . . . one of an old man praying over a small loaf of bread. Grace.

As mother to four sons, I knew this was not uncommon behavior for a curious preschooler. What was uncommon, was the length of time he stood still.

"Whatch' doing honey?" I asked.

"Looking." He said the word as if it were heavy.

Moving closer, I noticed tears forming under the long, dark lashes—not unusual for this particular son, the most tender-hearted of our brood.

"What are you thinking?"

He didn't even hesitate with his answer.

"He doesn't have any peanut butter."

—**Mary Bahr Fritts**

A Mother's Heart

A mother's heart is born long before the baby is.
A mother's heart comes with built-in elastic
to stretch wider for each child,
to bounce back each time her child disappoints her,
to grow greater in patience when her child requires it.
A mother's heart weeps often and long,
feeling each hurt as if it were her own,
knowing each fault as if it were her own.

A mother's heart may get tired,
but it never gives up.
A mother's heart is her child's own private
cheering section, believing
when no one else believes,understanding
when no one else understands, loving
when no one else can.

A mother's heart knows her child's a winner
when no one else knows.
A mother's heart will win in the end
for the love of it will win in the heart of the child,
Which, being filled so often with it,
finally sees it for what it is,
The sweet pouring-out of God's own love
for as long as it takes
as much as it takes,
the message, a single melody, the ceaseless refrain—
"You are worth something,
You are forever loved,
You are somebody,
You are forever Mine."
Until finally the heart of the child believes the mother's heart.

—Lynell Gray

Hippie Days Are Here . . . Again?

"I'm going to be a hippie for Halloween this year," My sixteen-year-old daughter, Jaimee, announced, pulling down the ladder stairs leading to the attic. "Do you have any old bell-bottoms?"

I shook my head, remembering tripping over too-wide bell-bottoms while my husband-to-be roared with laughter. What was this challenging teenager up to now?

"I think Dad used those for grease rags years ago," I answered.

As she disappeared into the attic, I reflected on the outgoing little girl I once cuddled in my lap. In her place was this headstrong teenager who wanted privileges I wasn't ready to give.

Help me, Lord, I'd pray, *I don't know what to do with her.* I grounded her often, rarely believed what she told me, and checked up on her everywhere she went. *Was I this difficult to raise?* I wondered.

Jaimee descended from the attic with a skirt I'd made for her when she was about five years old and was an Indian girl for Halloween. I eyed the striped colors warily.

"Don't you think it's too short?" I suggested. She grinned, green eyes twinkling.

"Well," I sighed, shaking my head in resignation, "Wear your cheerleading tights underneath."

"What kind of shoes should I wear with it?" She was off and running now. For once I hadn't expressed disapproval. I thought about the black suede platform shoes I'd bought when I was a young, slim thing. For a moment I almost regretted giving those impractical style statements to *Goodwill.*

"What about boots?" she asked, interrupting my reverie. She took off through the house in search of footwear and came back with a pair of black, combat-style hunting boots.

"Would these work?" she asked, pulling one on.

Her older brother Todd sneered. "Hippies burned those things back then," he informed her, his voice dripping with sarcastic authority. "They *protested* war, remember?"

"Oh," she said, ignoring his aren't-you-the-idiot tone and dropping the boot on the dining room floor.

While Jaimee dug into a pile of shoes, Todd opened the coat closet and pulled out a worn, brown suede jacket with a matching satin lining.

"Here," he said, thrusting it at her, "If you really want to look like a hippie, wear this!"

She slipped it over her black, form-fitting jersey.

"That's the *perfect* finishing touch!" I exclaimed, scrutinizing her brown leather sandals, Indian-style miniskirt and matching headband. She grinned and held up both hands in a peace sign. Silky, chestnut hair fell to her shoulders and framed her dimpled cheeks.

Did I look like that? I wondered. *Everyone says she looks just like me when I was her age.*

"Do you remember where I got that jacket?" my husband interrupted.

"Tijuana, Mexico, when you were in the service," I answered, remembering a frosty, moonlit hay ride and the smell of new leather and old hay mixed.

I'd met him a couple months after his discharge. By then he'd grown a beard and sported wavy, shoulder-length hair. I fell in love with him when he smiled and his blue eyes twinkled. But my mother doubted that this tall, shaggy man who took me for long rides on his Harley Davidson sportster was the man for me—until she saw the twinkle in his eyes when she confessed looking for needle marks on his arm.

"I need some hippie jewelry," Jaimee announced. "Do you have any beads? What kind of earrings did they wear?" She spun around and scooted upstairs, returning with one gold earring dangling from one ear and a big, gold hoop in the other.

"Which ones?" she asked.

"The dangly ones," I answered.

"The big hoops," offered her dad. "I think I have a peace sign necklace around here that you could wear."

I rolled my eyes. Now *he* was getting in the act! But then, wasn't it fun? For once mother and daughter weren't locking horns. Caught up in the excitement of dressing her up, I remembered what it was like to be young and struggling to find my own identity. The years melted away, and it was I who stood before scrutinizing parents.

"Please, give me the freedom to make my own mistakes!" My own words echoed in my daughter's eyes. Now I was the one holding on too tightly. *Just love her,* God was telling me. *Rejoice in the person she is becoming.*

"Yes," I smiled at my hippie-wanna-be, "A peace sign would be just perfect."

—Michele T. Huey

"I'm grounded. I said one more word to my mother."

A Queen Indeed

I tucked her in,
my little girl;
Her arms raised sweetly as if to encircle me,
But I brushed them aside, gave her a peck on the cheek
For I was thinking of chores yet to be done,
And I was tired.
As I hastened to leave—she spoke.
"You look like a queen,
Mommy."
I stood staring at the rug.
Yet not even seeing the fabric of it,
Seeing instead my sloppy slippers
curlered hair,
hastily-donned housecoat;
And I turned back to hug
and to kiss
my little princess.
What are a few moments
to a stack of dirty dishes
or a pile of rumpled clothes?
I thought.
And who can be tired when they
rule a kingdom of the heart?

—**Unknown**

It Is Well

"Go to sleep right now and I'd better not hear another word out of you two," I yelled. "You hear me?"

"Y-e-e-s, Mommy," my six-year-old son, Kyle, wept, his face pressing downward into his pillow.

"Mommy, Mommy," wailed my three-year-old.

"Erika! Be quiet." I snapped, slamming their bedroom door behind me. "I can't take this anymore! "I yanked the rubberband off my ponytail, tossing it furiously across the bathroom counter.

"This place is a disaster!" I yelled, bolting down the hallway, hurling piles of dirty clothes into the white basket by the living room stairs.

"I'm tired of this. I need my space," I muttered, staggering into the kitchen. "It's the same routine every day. Crying, whining, fighting. Sometimes I feel like my life would be better off without them. I could be on my computer for hours, doing what I love most. Or reading a book. Or working out," I angrily thought, kicking the pantry door with full force, loosening it from its hinges.

"Where's my husband when I need him? I hate all the hours he works."

Exhausted, my body collapsed in front of the damaged door. "Oh, Lord, help," I pleaded. "Please do a miracle with my husband's graveyard schedule. I need him home at nights to help me with the kids.

"Get a hold of yourself," I thought, choking with shame. "Your children are gifts from God. Now go back in there and apologize to them." Silence engulfed the house as I slowly made my way back into their room.

"Mommy loves you, Kyle," I softly whispered, caressing his dark brown hair and gazing into his big brown eyes.

"I love you too, Mommy," he tearfully replied.

Bending over to the lower bunk bed, I stared at my three-year-old's fragile little body, thumb in mouth, sniffling as she slept.

"Erika, I'm so sorry. Mommy loves you very much. One day, you and I will be best of friends." I sobbed uncontrollably, gently wiping off tear drops that still rested upon her porcelain cheeks; her long brown hair drenched with sweat.

Morning arrived and I suddenly felt a surge of joy eroding last night's fatigue. "Lord, give me a freshness on life and motherhood this morning. Give me strength to endure another day."

As I helped Kyle get dressed for school, I randomly popped in an Odyssey Adventure audio tape into his player. The story progressed as I listened intently.

"I'm sorry sir, the telegram has just arrived. Your wife and daughters . . . the ship went down in twelve minutes . . ." the narrator regretfully announced.

"Dear God, my heart is so heavy. My children, my precious children. Give me strength to bear the pain."

My throat tightened and my heart began to ache as I felt this father's anguish.

"This man, H.G. Stafford, had not only lost his wife and four daughters in a sinking ship, but also his only son to pneumonia, years earlier. And some time after visiting the sea site of his family's sunken ship," the narrator continued, "He was able, even through his ordeal, to write one of the most inspirational songs of all time, 'It Is Well With My Soul'."

Tears flooded down my cheeks as I glanced at Kyle, and then at Erika. "Oh, Lord," I humbly prayed in my heart, hugging my little girl, "I'm so sorry for my selfish behavior. Please forgive me. I have no right to treat them as an inconvenience. Here's a man who loved his children and lost them all. Oh, what would I do if that should ever happen to me? Please, Lord, continue to remind me that Kyle and Erika are gifts from You. No matter how difficult this season of my life may be, teach me to always sing in my heart, 'It is well, with my soul'."

—Therese A. Robertson

11

Outreach

". . . but you shall receive power when the Holy Spirit has come upon you; and you shall be My witnesses both in Jerusalem and in all Judea and Samaria, and even to the remotest part of the earth."

Acts. 1:8

A Child's Scream

I was so angry, I marched across Maple Street without once thinking of the consequences. The woman who had recently moved into the little rental tucked between two older, more-established residents was constantly hurling obscenities at her young child. The poor little girl's screams broke the silence of our quiet neighborhood and the peace of my heart as well. I planned to tell the mother a thing or two about how awful she was.

It didn't take me long to pick my way across the cluttered yard and knock on the battered screen door of the tiny house. A sad young woman with big brown eyes answered. Suddenly, I was lost in those eyes. They were swollen and red from crying, and dark circles formed rings of frustration on a face that silently screamed for relief. "I . . . I . . . I heard the crying," I stammered. ". . . thought you might need some help."

Although we had never even met each other, she fell sobbing into my arms. Her thin shoulders jerked against my body as I silently prayed to God for insight. Looking beyond her into the darkness of the house, I caught a glimpse of another set of sad brown eyes peeking from behind the bedroom door.

Instead of telling the young mother how awful she was, I spent the next couple of hours listening as she shared her story over steaming cups of cinnamon tea. In the months to come she and her daughter spent more time at my house than theirs. We made cookies together, sang songs, and learned to have fun. In the process, both Jenny and Jessica learned of God's love and grace.

I learned something about the power of God's love and grace as well. I John 3:20 says, "For God is greater than our hearts, and he knows everything." (NIV) Truly, His love overpowered my anger as He knew best how to meet the needs of the young mother and daughter in the little rental house across Maple Street.

—**Sandy Cathcart**

Setting Myself Aside

I stepped to the bookstore counter with several "how to" books on evangelism. I hoped that these books would help me overcome the fear that makes me tongue-tied when I have an opportunity to speak out for Jesus.

As I waited, I stood next to a young man affected by what appeared to be cerebral palsy. He waved his arms while talking excitedly to the clerk about his girlfriend. It was difficult to understand his slurred speech. "Just last night she . . . She . . . Accep . . . ted Je . . . Jesus!" he exclaimed. He wanted to buy some self-stick letters and posterboard to make a large sign with a Bible verse to encourage her.

When the clerk responded with a puzzled expression, the young man pointed to a Bible on the shelf. The clerk handed it to him. He opened it and, in a clear voice, read Isaiah 41:13: "I, the Lord your God, hold your right hand; it is I who say to you, 'Fear not, I will help you'." Then, turning to Exodus 4:12, he continued, "Go, and I will be with your mouth and teach you what you shall speak." Those of us standing nearby listened in amazement as he read God's Word without stuttering.

Although I had come prepared to buy the books in my hand, I no longer needed them in the same way. At that moment I realized that the support for which I had searched had been with me all along. God requires a willing heart to respond to his directive, "Go."

As God prepared Moses and Isaiah—and the young man at the counter—God prepares me. I continually learn to set myself aside and to rely only on Him. When my heart and life focus on God, He enables me, through the power of his Holy Spirit, to open my mouth and speak out for Jesus.

—**Mary K. Kasting**

Anita, The Eskimo Girl

She came into my apartment with a smile as broad as Broadway. I noticed her sneakers were tattered and open at the toe. I wondered how she could stand to be outside in such weather. It was 60 below with a wind chill factor of 100 degrees below zero!

I was a nursing teacher who had gone to teach a selected group of teen-aged Eskimo (Inuit) girls a ward aide course. They came from places with exotic names like Rankin Inlet, Eskimo Point, Baker Lake, Chesterfield Inlet, Coral Harbor and others. I ushered her into my apartment where we met with several other girls each week to talk and to study the Bible. I had gone there to teach them but I came away having been taught by them.

Anita was different right from the start. She had a sunny disposition and a faith that taught me a lot. Often she came early to tell me about her experiences with God. It was obvious she loved Him with all her heart. She had a child-like faith that He was always with her to provide for her every need. She was truly without guile. God said it. He was real. Therefore she simply believed it. She had not been taught otherwise!

As we sat there waiting for the other students to arrive, I suddenly remembered that I had a second pair of winter boots in my closet. That week another Eskimo girl had presented me with a pair of home-made sealskin mukluks which I had bought from her. I wore them most of the time and had no need of another pair of boots.

I stared at Anita's feet. I knew her foot size without even asking! Quietly I went to my closet and retrieved the boots and simply handed them to her.

"These belong to you, I think." I said.

Silently she put them on and smiled.

"I asked Jesus to give me a pair of boots," she said simply.

She thanked me but her thanks were directed to the God she so trusted.

As for me, I'm glad I obeyed that inner urge to simply hand over the boots, one of my favorite pair and expensive too! I learned a lot from Anita!

—Arlene Rudd Centerwall

SEEKING SANCTUARY

RIGHT before our family vacation, my husband and I decided to transfer our children from a Christian school to a public one. While traveling, our seven-year old daughter, Andrea, announced she needed to use the bathroom. When we stopped at the gas station, my husband went to inquire about their facilities, but returned to explain they didn't have any public restrooms. Desperately, Andrea pleaded, "Oh Daddy, please go ask if they have any Christian ones!"

—Pierrette M. Begent

Why All The Fuss Over One Banana?

My three-year-old granddaughter, Victoria, and I joined the checkout line with our hoard of hot rolls, cold cuts, fresh fruit and chocolate ice cream for a lunch we would soon share with her parents at their home nearby.

A neatly-dressed, elderly gentleman who could not speak English silently presented one cold drink, one banana and some food stamps to the young clerk. Grabbing the banana, the boy plopped it on the scale and then shaking his head "no," handed it back to the man.

Patiently, the elder left the line, banana in hand, and headed back to the produce section. As I watched nearby, he gently replaced the banana before beginning a search for a different one.

After making his selection, the man scurried back to the checkout where the clerk once again weighed the single banana, shook his head and shoved it back across the counter. Undaunted, the "would be customer" picked up the banana and headed back to find a replacement.

Curiosity got the best of me and in a near whisper, I asked him why this old gentleman was being bounced back and forth like a tennis ball. All the while, the frowning store owner posted inches from the clerk's elbow, did not utter a word.

With a helpless shrug of the shoulders, the boy nervously explained that each of the bananas the man selected weighed too much so that when totaled with the cold drink, his food stamps fell short.

Trying to control my outrage, I dragged a squealing Victoria to the banana counter. A quick study of the display disclosed no distinctive difference in the size of the bananas, certainly not enough to justify the indignities to which this gentle elder was being subjected. Why all the fuss over one banana? It made no sense, not even from a business viewpoint, considering the inconvenience to the other customers waiting in line.

But there did seem to be a simple solution. Still trying to quell my anger, I grabbed a big bunch of bananas and brought them up to the clerk just as the old man was being ordered out on another search mission. Touching the man's arm, I motioned him to wait. Then sliding a bunch of bananas onto the counter beside my own items, I told the clerk to bag them for the man and charge them to my order.

Taken by surprise, the grandpa turned to face me with a raised eyebrow. For a brief moment, our eyes locked. Not a word was exchanged, only nodding heads and smiles which provided an umbrella of mutual understanding and respect. I watched as he exited the store to be greeted by three excited youngsters jumping up and down, reaching for the goodies.

Inside the store, one customer frustrated by the delay remarked, "I wonder why he was so fussy about picking out one little banana?"

The store owner joined in, "I wonder why he can't come in here with enough money to pay for what he wants."

I dropped my head, silently berating myself wondering why I didn't buy him more bananas.

—Jean Rodgers

Greater Works Shall We Do

Four years ago, I attended the California's Inland Empire Prayer Convention. While in my prayer cluster, I felt the urging of the Holy Spirit to exhort according to Matthew 25:35-36, ". . . shelter the homeless, feed the poor, clothe the naked, visit the lonely . . . for to the extent that we do this unto the least of our brothers, we do it unto Jesus." Tears welled in my eyes, as well as those around me.

The following week, the admonition lingered on my mind. So I devised a plan. Every Thursday I decided to bring five sack lunches with me to work. At twelve noon, I went out on my own, walked a few blocks, and gave out bags to the homeless.

At the time I was a probation officer submitting sentencing recommendations to the Superior Court in downtown San Bernardino. Afraid I might meet one of the offenders I'd once recommended serve three years in state prison (and was only ordered 60 days in county jail), I decided I shouldn't do this alone.

I called a couple of friends and encouraged them to meet me at a nearby restaurant on Saturday morning and bring five lunches, individually sacked. They showed up, we prayed, and within the hour, whether in a ditch, through the window of an abandoned car, or behind a dumpster, we fed a meal to fifteen homeless, being sure to include a kind word.

It's been over five years now and we haven't missed a Saturday yet. The money, labor, and time spent is still our own. We are about fourteen people strong, which means about seventy lunches. Combine this with the power of Jesus through our prayers, we feed anywhere from three-to-four-thousand people a year, plus share the gospel with a tract or by word. That's 14,000 lunches throughout our history. For He promised, ". . . greater works than these shall (you) do . . ."

One of the remarkable aspects of our outreach is that four of our team used to be men we fed in the park a couple of years back. Since they have gained employment, a home, and transportation, they have come back to help. One particular gentleman, while living at the men's shelter, came faithfully with either bananas or cokes to add to our bags. One time I gave him a brand new pair of socks which he hid in his back waistband. A little later that day, we were handing a lunch to a homeless man. He looked at us and said, "What I really need is a pair of socks." The helper, without hesitation, pulled from his waistband the new socks and handed it to the man. This is what giving is about!

—Anesa C. Cronin

Finding God On Ice

One cold January evening, John, my college sophomore, sauntered into the steamy kitchen where I was preparing dinner.

"I'm thinking about joining the hockey team at school," he blurted out.

Twenty years of parenting had sensitized me to the kids' signals indicating the need for a sounding board. So I turned from the stove to join him at the kitchen table where he sat nibbling on a carrot stick.

"Sounds like a great idea," I baited, hoping to learn more details.

Actually, I harbored some misgivings about his ability to play hockey at the college level, because part-time jobs had always cut into the practice time required to excel. But John loved hockey so much that he wouldn't give up on it, doing the best he could with the time and talents he had.

As though reading my mind, he continued, "I know I don't have much of a chance to make the team; but I'd even settle for bench warmer. At least I'd be sure to have a front-row season seat!"

"Then go for it!" I blurted out.

Over the following weeks, I prayed for affirmation that I was right to encourage John's decision. On one occasion I even invited John to join me in prayer; as part of his preparation for upcoming tryouts.

"Like God doesn't have more important things to take care of," he snapped.

"Don't knock it if you ain't tried it," I teased, reverting to my standard line of reproach in such situations with the kids.

The next time we talked, I suggested to John that he "converse with Jesus as you would a good friend—and do it at work, on the ice or during the dash between classes."

Surprisingly, this time John nodded in agreement. After all, a few unexpected signs of encouragement had come his way lately, including compliments from the coach on his enthusiasm and team spirit. Privately, he pondered whether the ragged, informal prayer talks he had been having with God were the reason for the coach's support.

But then one evening he returned home from an especially rough practice session—convinced that he was in over his head. I talked him into remaining, pledging my continuing prayer support, and again inviting him to pray.

"You never give up do you, Mom?" he said sadly.

"Don't knock it if you ain't tried it," I persisted, unaware of his initial prayer attempts.

Then, about a week later, John came bursting in the door to announce he had made the team.

My husband and I were overjoyed. Besides making the team, we noted a growing respect for the power of prayer, since John went about applying it to other challenges coming his way academically, socially and in the working-world.

But it was during a crucial hockey game against a top competitor, when John's team was down two players and two goals with a scant six minutes left in the game, that we saw the best results.

Even though we couldn't hear them, from our spectator seats my husband and I detected something serious going on between John and the boy beside him on the bench. John apparently was carrying on a one-man rally for his team-mates, jumping up and down, fists waving. The boy beside him suddenly jumped up too, but it wasn't to cheer. Instead, tossing his stick aside in anger, he gave John a shove and then got right in his face screaming something.

John took a step back, gazing calmly at the boy. Then with a shrug of the shoulders, John said something to him that triggered a grimace of disbelief.

Suddenly a sea of screams flooded the arena: "Score! Score!"

Both John and his bench-mate turned their attention back to the ice. The opposition's battered goalie lost his balance, enabling two more fantastic plays that outwitted the clock, and carried John's team to victory.

After the game, John shared with us his "prayer encounter"

on the bench. It seems the other boy screamed at John to sit down and shut up. "It's all over, we can't do anything."

"We can pray," John shot back.

When the boy turned from him, my beloved prayer student persisted, "Don't knock it if you ain't tried it."

I shivered at the awareness of God's affirmation that he cares not about style, form or circumstance. God is always there for us, even if the setting is as unconventional as two boys heatedly debating God's power in the midst of a rowdy, ice skating arena.

—Jean Rodgers

12

Prayer

Be anxious for nothing, but in everything by prayer and supplication, with thanksgiving, let your requests be made known to God.

Philippians 4:6

The Problem

I stood in the upstairs hallway and looked down over the banister. As I waited for the younger children to come in for their baths, my oldest daughter was taking a piano lesson in the living room directly below. The repetitive melody she was playing echoed through my mind. Standing there, I savored both the few moments of solitude and the aroma from the roast beef and apple pie already in the oven.

Suddenly the little ones bounded through the door. I cringed as I saw their muddy footprints on the white carpet and their filthy little hands leaving distinct imprints on the cream-colored walls. They bounced up to their rooms, cheeks flushed and eyes bright from their play.

I noticed, however, that one of my young sons was trudging slowly up the stairs, his head bowed, grubby hands covering his small, dirt-streaked face. When he reached the top, I asked him what was wrong.

"Aw, nothing," he replied.

"Then why are you holding your face in your hands?"

"Oh, I was just praying."

Quite curious now, I asked what he was praying about.

"I can't tell you," he insisted, "Because if I do, you'll be mad."

After much persuasion I convinced him he could confide in me and that, whatever he told me, I would not get mad. So he explained that he was praying about a problem he had with his mind.

"A problem with your mind?" I asked, now more curious than ever. What kind of problem could a six-year old have with his mind?

"Well," he said, "Every time I pass by the living room, I see my piano teacher, and my tongue sticks out."

Hard as it was to keep a straight face, I took his problem seriously and assured him that God could, indeed, help him with it.

Later, on my knees beside the bathtub as I bathed this little fellow, I thought how I still struggle with the problem of controlling my mind and my tongue. All too often my mind focuses on the negative until negativism dominates my thoughts and actions. I find myself being critical and unpleasant. Repeatedly I realize that I have said what I didn't mean to say, and haven't said what I really wanted to say—such as, "Thank you" or, "Well done!" or even, "I love you." All too often I focus on faults, while ignoring or forgetting the much-needed word of praise, encouragement, or appreciation.

That afternoon as I knelt to scrub that sturdy little body, the tub became my altar; the bathroom, my temple. I bowed my head, covered my face, and acknowledged that I, like my son, had a problem with my mind and tongue. I asked the Lord to forgive me and to give me more and more the mind and heart of Christ.

—Gigi Graham Tchividjian

A Goofy Prayer

In 1981 I made a goofy and ridiculous prayer request. I was 19 years old, a new believer and naive to say the least. I prayed, "Lord, I want to see my face on a billboard." At that time, I was an airheaded twin model and actress, struggling to make a living in Los Angeles, California. Most of my work was with my twin sister. We were one of the many sets of DOUBLEMINT twins.

A few years later, with my prayer request long forgotten, I was on a bus in Zurich, Switzerland. I had just finished filming a German hair commercial. My face pressed against the bus window, I stared out into the dark sky. Moments later, I screamed. The bus driver slammed on his brakes. I pointed at a nearby billboard and shouted, "There I am." The bus driver shouted some musical sounding German expletives. I didn't care that I was making a fool of myself. I was overcome with unbelief as I snapped pictures of my COKE smiling face, gracing the sky of Zurich. Then, a still small voice whispered in my ear, "I heard your request." I looked heavenward and felt the awesome presence of God in this faded-red, littered bus, smelling of stale cigarettes and perspiration. It was a holy and thankful moment. I didn't want it to end.

Looking back on that event years later, what shocked me more than seeing my contrived smiling face in that "COKE Adds Life" moment, was the reality of how thankless I am. Why does it take an extraordinary answer to a goofy prayer request to motivate me to praise Him with a passionate heart? God seemed more alive to me in that Zurich moment, than any Sunday morning worship and praise service. He surprised me in an incredible way. Perhaps we all need to pray more goofy prayers.

Seventeen years later, I was to be surprised by God again—this time when I hadn't even prayed any goofy prayer. Late one night in the summer of '96, my husband watched David Letterman on TV. I read upstairs with heavy eyelids, sleep fast approaching.

My tranquillity was sharply shattered by my hubby's shouting and mumbled voice. My mind panicked. *Oh no! he's choking on pizza!* With the energy of my kids on Christmas morning, I scrambled out of bed and jumped down the stairs two-by-two. As I hit the bottom stair, I lost my balance and stubbed my toe. "What's going on?" I shouted. I felt the pain from my toe ignite a glance of anger at my husband.

He wildly pointed and exclaimed, "Look honey, you're on television!"

I glanced at Letterman's gap-tooth smiling face. Much to my shock, in his right hand, he held an album cover with my "COKE Adds Life" grin. I looked heavenward and then back at the television and thought, *Lord, you have an incredible sense of humor and timing.*

Letterman chatted about the COKE music while making fun of the lyrics and I pondered why that dated image keeps popping up, even after eleven years of marriage, two kids and graying hair. I also remembered the Zurich moment, my overwhelming and humbling experience of His presence in that faded-red, littered bus.

Reality snapped back as my image faded into a commercial break. Returning to bed with my sore toe and stunned heart, I thought about my contrived COKE image. Ironically, it has become my monument of God's faithfulness, despite my often thankless and grumbling heart in refusing to passionately worship Him. Once again, He winked at me through the icon of our age and reminded me of His presence and humor in the seemingly mundane moments of life.

—Vanessa Craig

Praying Without Words

When I entered the darkness of the church's auditorium, I wasn't sure why I had come. My kids were attending youth group several buildings away and I felt drawn to sit there as I pondered my anguish over several friends at church. Thinking about one of them, a man with a terminal disease, I sat in his usual chair on the right side of the auditorium. There in the darkness I tried to pray for him but words would not come. So I sat there and grieved for him. I found myself hunched over, elbows on my knees, head in my hands, as he always sat. I knew I was praying for him, but I couldn't tell you what I said.

After a few minutes, I moved across the room to the seat where another friend usually sat. She felt betrayed by another church member and was crumbling inside, but didn't want anyone to know it. I sat upright and tall in her chair, as she always did. She often wore a look on her face that said, "I'm going forth! Watch out!" and so did I as I sat in wordless prayer for her.

Finally, I moved toward the center aisle into the seat of a friend who was separated from his wife. He always extended his arm across the empty chair next to him as if he were waiting for her to sit there, and I did the same. As I felt his grief, it became clear to me that each of them felt rejected by God in some way. My prayer found these words: "Help them know You love them."

It was then I realized that it wasn't smart to sit alone in a building in the dark in a gangland neighborhood. What had driven me to sit there? I had prayed so much for these friends for weeks that a little prayer sprinkled here and there was no longer enough. The time had come to agonize in the dark for them, to focus on them in a determined way.

After a while I left to run some errands, and when I went to pick up my kids, I saw the lights on in the auditorium. I tiptoed in and there sat one of the men I had prayed for, playing the piano. I hesitated, then walked toward him, leaned over and said,

"You are loved desperately by God." His face looked blank, but his eyes filled. "That's exactly what I need to hear," he said.

—Jan Johnson

UP IN ARMS

DURING a recent Sunday worship service, our congregation sang the chorus. "I exalt thee, oh Lord . . ." As I sang, I glanced down at my five-year-old daughter standing beside me. Her little arms were up in the air and she was singing, "I'm exhausted, oh Lord . . ."

—Sandy Anthony

Lessons On Love

I got out of the car, my arms loaded down with books. As I closed the car door with my backside, I looked down at the ground. The fragile new grass growing along the dirt path awakened childhood memories. It had been a hard day and I was hurting. I wasn't eager to go inside. There was no one in the house I could share my hurt with, no adult I could talk to. My two precious sons were there, but they were not to be my confidants. I was their Mother. I was their parent—a single parent. My husband was dead.

The grass reminded me of Grandpa's cabin at the lake. For an instant it had looked like the grass on the path leading down to the rickety old dock, and I remembered the time I fell into the water and somehow came up under the dock, choking and scared. Daddy took me in his arms and held me while I cried, brushing back the wet hair that had escaped my pigtails and now covered my eyes. When my sobbing stopped, he convinced me to get back into the water.

I loved my daddy's arms and welcomed any opportunity to be in them. When I'd skin my knees-which was frequently for this tomboy—I'd run to Daddy. Or in the evenings, sometime between doing the dishes and my homework, I'd often curl up in his lap, lean my head on his chest, and feel so secure.

The grass and my present hurt reminded me of all that. How I wished I were a little girl again. I wished I had someone to hold me right now, to tell me that everything would be all right and reassure me that I'd survive.

As I turned to walk into the house, I suddenly saw in my mind's eye a little girl in pigtails flying down a vast marble corridor. Oil paintings bigger than life hung on the walls. As she ran, I could almost hear her little shoes on the marble floor. Tears flooded her eyes and overflowed, leaving white streaks on her dirty face. Blood trickled down her skinned leg, making a path in the dirt and gravel embedded in her knee and shin. She was calling for her daddy and sobbing as she ran.

It was a long corridor. At the end, two huge gold doors glistened in the sunlight which filtered through beveled cathedral windows. On either side of the imposing doors stood two magnificently-dressed guards holding huge spears and blocking the entrance into the room beyond.

Undaunted, the little girl ran straight toward the doors, still crying, "Abba!" She never broke her stride for, as she neared the doors, the guards flung them open and heralded her arrival: "The daughter of the King! The daughter of the King!"

Court was in session. The cherubim and seraphim cried, "Holy, holy, holy!," and the elders sat on their thrones, dressed in white, wearing crowns of gold, and talking with the King of Kings. But none of this slowed down His daughter!

Oblivious to everything going on about her, she ran past the seven burning lamps of fire and up the steps leading to the throne, and she catapulted herself into the King's arms. She was home and wrapped in the arms of His everlasting love. He reached up and, with one finger, gently wiped away her tears. Then He smoothed the sticky hair on her face back into her braids, tenderly held her leg, and said, "Now, now, tell your Father all about it."

I walked into my house, went to my bedroom, and got on my knees.

Never once have I had a hard time telling my heavenly Father all about it. Never once have I feared He would push me away. My daddy never did and neither did my mother, so why would God?

—Kay Arthur

From Bypass To God's Peace

"Herb, wake up!" Zeliah whispered again and again. "Please wake up." Zeliah Kleinfeld held her husband, Herb's, hand and glanced in bewilderment at the monitors with their zigzag lines like continuous flashes of lightning.

It had been three days since Herb's bypass surgery and he still hadn't regained consciousness. Zeliah thought back to a week ago when the doctor first told her, "Zeliah, Herb needs bypass surgery." It took awhile for his words to penetrate. *Heart surgery! What if my husband dies?* Her own heart beat crazily.

Herb's positive attitude had surprised Zeliah. She was the one with the apprehension. Feeling no peace, she thought, "What would I do without him if he didn't make it?"

A short week later, Herb's sons, Jerry and Richard, were with her when the doctor appeared after six hours of surgery.

"Zeliah, Jerry, Richard, sit down," he motioned them back to their seats. "Herb is now in the Cardiac Care Unit. The surgery was much worse than we anticipated. We performed a quadruple bypass and repaired an aneurysm. It was a miracle that it hadn't ruptured, but Herb held his own."

They waited and waited—two hours—three—four. The nurse always answered, "He hasn't come to yet."

Toward morning Jerry and Richard insisted driving Zeliah home. She felt exhausted. "We'll call you the minute you can get in to see Dad," they promised.

No call came but the next morning they came for her. The nurses allowed Zeliah to see Herb for a few minutes but he still hadn't regained consciousness. She clasped Herb's hand, so warm and familiar, but it didn't return her pressure. "Oh, Lord," Zeliah breathed, "How long?"

When she left the room, she found a phone and called a friend in her Bible class and requested prayer. In her numbness she found it hard to pray more than a sentence or two.

On the third day, Herb showed no signs of ever rousing. Finally on the tenth day the doctor took all of them aside and said, "I'm sorry to tell you this, but Herb isn't going to recover. He's been in a coma too long. His brain must have lacked oxygen during the surgery. Even if he responds now he will surely show brain damage."

The room suddenly seemed to tilt sideways for Zeliah. "Oh, God, where are You? Why haven't You heard and answered our prayers?"

The next two days she stayed home from the hospital. The doctors had consulted and spoke of turning off the machines in another 48 hours if there was no change. Zeliah couldn't face being there when it happened.

She called her friend, Jo, from the Bible class to tell her how hopeless it seemed. Jo refused to give up. "It is not impossible with God! The doctors aren't God!"

As promised, Jo led prayer at the Bible class. "Lord, we know You can wake up Herb and restore Him to good health, but Lord, however, You answer, we pray that You will give Zeliah your peace."

As Zeliah made her bed, she saw Herb's clothes hanging in the closet next to hers. Tears flowed. The thought of a possible funeral was more than she could wrestle with at that moment.

She sat on the edge of her bed and opened her Bible. It had been neglected, she realized, when she needed it most. A verse underlined in Isaiah 26:3 stood out boldly. "Thou wilt keep him in perfect peace, whose mind is stayed on Thee." God's peace flowed through her being. *Whatever the outcome, I know it will be all right.*

Two weeks after Herb's surgery, God's peace still surrounded her.

Zeliah waited for the call from the hospital that she knew had to come sooner or later. When the phone finally rang, she sat down and took a long breath before answering. She lifted the receiver and recognized the doctor's voice. "Hey, Zeliah, Herb woke up! Come on down!"

God had answered their prayers! *But Herb might have brain damage*, the thought flashed through Zeliah's mind, but somehow she knew the God who could wake him up, would make him completely well.

One month later Herb walked out of the hospital. Now less than a year later he is bowling, driving and doing almost everything he ever did. Today as Zeliah sees their clothes hanging side by side in their closet, she pauses and praises God anew. "Oh, Lord, Your peace remains a daily reality."

—Mary Lou Klingler

God Calling

The first time He called,
the phone was busy.
He called back
and got the machine—
I was home, but I wanted to see
What He had to say first . . .
He tried me at work,
But I put Him on call screening,
Then call forward.

One time He placed a long-distance,
three-way, conference call
With my conscience on the other line.

He sat on hold for a long time,
And my conscience stayed on,
But I hung up.

He just could not get through.

But then I got sick.
Really sick.
And I wanted Him to call right away.
But He didn't!
So I called Him. Long distance. Collect.
I got a recording,
"This phone's been disconnected . . ."
I kept hitting the redial button
Over and over again.

I was desperate.
So I went to talk to Pastor.

Pastor told me my wires were messed up.
He said I had to straighten them out
And get a new connection.

So I did.
And now my calls go straight through.
And He answers every time.

But He still has trouble getting through to me—
Sometimes I don't hear the phone ring.
And then something goes wrong,
and I realize how long He's been trying to get through to me.
So now I have the volume turned up.

Make sure you're listening for His call,
Because if you answer His,
He'll answer yours every time.

—**Debora Allen**

Sunday Morning

The doctor told my family that I might not live through the night. *Why did the doctor stay in the room to tell them. Didn't he know I heard every word?*

I wanted to clench my fists and yell. *Why can't you hear me? I'm not ready to leave yet. Lord, please bring me back.*

I laid in a coma for three days, unable to communicate. I did commune with God in a unique way. I felt His presence, and walked with Him. I heard the everyday chatter from nurses, and sensed when it was morning or night by the shift changes.

Three days earlier, like any typical Monday morning, I had prepared to leave for work. But a headache increased in pain over an hour and I decided to rest awhile. Even after taking an aspirin, the pain grew in intensity. *Something's wrong. This is no normal migraine headache.* Crawling to the phone in the kitchen, I dialed 911. The next thing I remember a medical team was helping me into a wheel chair. My head felt as if it would explode.

After numerous CT scans and examinations, the doctors decided that I had a subarachnoid hemorrhage. They scheduled surgery. Soon, I lapsed into a coma.

In the coma state, I still heard footsteps when someone entered my room and voices of people talking. I felt a doctor pinch my cheek, and poke me with needles hoping I would respond. I felt my husband's hand squeeze mine, but could not acknowledge his presence.

When I heard the doctor advise my husband and daughter of the fact that I might not survive the night, I wanted to scream at them, "No, no, I will be fine. I know. God has assured me that I will come home to you. Can't you hear?"

I knew God's presence prevailed. His peace filled my subconscious. We had intimate conversations with each other. I pleaded, "Please, oh please, don't take me away just yet. I want to write. I want to live a long life with my husband, and see my daughter marry a Christian man." I felt, without question, that God's hand touched my forehead, and said, "It's O.K. I hear your prayer."

The sound of a push cart awakened me from a peaceful sleep. I knew it was morning because the lab nurse arrived precisely at 6:00 a.m. every morning to take my blood. She always talked to me, told me the time, and announced her arrival with a cheery "top of the morning to ya." Then she patted my arm trying to find a place to take more blood samples from an already bruised and battered arm.

I struggled to open my eyes. My eye lids felt heavy, as if pieces of tape had closed them shut. After a concentrated effort, my eye lids fluttered open. A beautiful blond nurse leaned over my arm and continued talking to me. Then, she glanced at me and drew back in surprise. "Lordy, lordy, you're awake," she exclaimed, and ran from my room.

She brought back several nurses who stood around my bed smiling and crying. One of the nurses came over and hugged me. "I've prayed for you, Shirley, the last three days." She held my hand and said, "Welcome back. Some three-day nap you had."

I knew God brought me back to life with a tremendous promise of healing. "What . . . what day is it?" I asked.

One of the nurses stepped up, grabbed my hand, and said, "Why, honey, it's Sunday morning, and what a special Sunday morning it is."

I took hold of her hand and begged her to call my husband and daughter. "Please, call them for me? I want them to come up and see me after church."

"After church? Honey, I think they will come over right now."

God answered my prayers—and those of many others—for healing in my life.

—Shirley A. Reynolds

Blessings From A Bump

"I can't stand up!" shouted our nine-year-old son, John.

"What's wrong? Did you get hurt?" I questioned as I ran across the camp's dining hall to the water fountain.

"Some big kid bumped me with his elbow because the pew was so crowded during Bible quizzing. When I jumped up to answer a question, he jumped up at the same time and his elbow hit my side. He didn't mean it. I wanted to tell you when it started hurting, but I knew you were teaching the girls' Bible class."

"Let's find Dad and get you to a doctor."

Soon we arrived at the emergency room of a small clinic in a nearby town. Within minutes the doctor determined John was bleeding internally, probably from a ruptured spleen. He would have to have emergency exploratory surgery. An ambulance would take him to the hospital, which was about a thirty-minute drive.

"I don't want an operation. Will they cut me with a knife?" John asked.

My husband, Jim, affectionately laid his hand on John's head. "Son, we don't know for sure what all has to be done, but let's pray and commit all of this to the Lord.

"Dear Father, we need Your help. We lift John to You and ask You to touch his body, relieve the pain, and restore him to health. We ask for Your peace. Thank You for what You are going to do. In Jesus' name. Amen."

Jim would ride in the ambulance with John. I would follow in the car after I went back to camp to change clothes and get some overnight necessities. As I walked toward the parking lot to find our car I felt so helpless. *Oh, God, will John be OK?*

As I unlocked the door of the car, I noticed the bumper sticker on the car in front of ours. It read, "God has everything under control."

Thank You, Lord, for that reminder.

Back at camp, staff members and campers assured me of their prayers. I felt as though I was on "holy ground." I saw eight boys and their counselor in a circle. They were praying for John. They had his Bear Lake Camp T-shirt. As each boy led in prayer, he held the shirt, then passed it on to the next.

John was "prepped" for surgery by the time I arrived. Dr. Walsh, the surgeon, met us at the door. "I examined John, and yes, he is bleeding internally. However, I ordered a second blood count and it showed the bleeding was slowing up, so I want to wait ten minutes and take another count. You may come in and stay with him until we take him up to the operating room."

Oh, Father, please stop the bleeding, I silently prayed as I walked over to John's bed.

After another ten minutes had passed, Dr. Walsh informed us they were going to wait on the surgery for an hour because the blood tests revealed that the bleeding had continued to subside.

Blood was taken every hour for the next five hours until we were finally told that surgery was not necessary. The spleen was apparently bruised, but not ruptured.

What instant relief and overwhelming joy! Truly, the Lord heard our prayers.

All week long we had taught the campers about prayer and that God cares about everything that happens to His children. The campers not only learned these truths from the Bible classes, but also experienced the blessing of answered prayer in a time of crisis.

—Barbara J. Hibschman

I Believe In Miracles

On one snowy winter day, my daughter, Marg, came to our home to bake cookies. Her friend, Dot, called. The tone of Dot's voice revealed the discouragement she felt. Would Marg come and spend the evening with her?

Marg promised she would. At four o'clock snow started to fall.

"Are you still going to see Dot?" I asked. "You know it takes an hour to get there in good weather. A couple inches of snow could fall by the time You are ready to go home."

"I'll go see what it looks like on the main roads." Marg said. "Then I'll decide whether to go to Dot's house or to my apartment."

I watched as she started down our hill. "God, protect my daughter," I prayed. I also prayed that should Marg go see her friend, she would be given wisdom on how to give encouragement,

The snow continued to fall. Later that evening, when worried thoughts entered my mind, I would ask the Lord to take over the situation. The Bible verse, "The angel of the Lord encampeth roundabout them that fear him and delivereth them" (Psalms. 34:7), came to mind.

At nine o'clock Marg called.

"I had no trouble with the snow," she said. "The main roads were not bad, so I went to see Dot." She told of how her friend was encouraged by the visit. "Then on my way home, my car stopped, all at once, without any warning."

"What did you do?" I asked.

"It's a good thing the car stopped," she explained, "Because as soon as the engine cut off, three full-grown deer walked out in front of the car. After they were across the road, the car started without any problem, and I was on my way."

"Did you have any more trouble with the car on the way home?" I wanted to know.

"None at all," she said.

I believe in answer to prayer. It's not every day we can expect cars to stop when animals decide to cross the highway, but I believe God is waiting to perform more surprises for us than we can think.

—Irene Horst

Pray For Mercy

After my grandchild, Katherine Nate, was born, for several days we did not know if she would live or die. The first evening after her birth I stood numbly peering through the glass into the Neonatal Intensive Care Unit where my son Matthew was tenderly stroking Kate's tiny little frame. A woman standing next to me started a conversation. Her child was in the same unit because of a difficult birth, but her little boy was now out of danger. She told me she was a Christian and believed her child's recovery was an answer to prayer.

All day I had tried to pray, but no words would come out. I couldn't gather my thoughts enough to pray and frankly, I wasn't too sure how I felt about God or if prayer did any good anyway. I asked this young mother, "How did you pray? What did you ask for?"

She answered, "Oh, honey, I just prayed for mercy. Whatever would be merciful, to let my child live or to let him die. That's what I wanted."

Then she added, "I'll pray for mercy for your Kate."

I muttered a weak "Thank you," but I really wasn't sure if prayer would help much.

Glen and I left Matthew and little Kate about 2 a.m. to drive home to San Bernardino where I washed, dried and packed some clothes while Glen caught a quick nap. About 6 a.m., we headed back to San Diego feeling weary and discouraged. It was our twenty-ninth wedding anniversary, but there didn't seem to be much to celebrate. Our granddaughter was clinging to life by a thread; we could possibly be attending a funeral within the next few days. Life seemed to take too much effort.

I wearily reached over and picked up a Bible which was laying on the car seat next to me. I don't really believe in the "hunt and peck" system of reading Scripture, but that day I basically dared God to give me a verse which would comfort me and I let the pages just drop open.

My eyes fell on Psalm 103 and I absentmindedly read until I came to verse 17: "But the mercy of the Lord is from everlasting to everlasting upon them that fear him, and his righteousness unto children's children." I focused on the words *mercy* and *children's children.* God was promising everlasting mercy to me and to my children's children—my Kate!

It was still many days before we knew Kate would live and many more months beyond that before we were certain there wasn't permanent brain damage, but during that time I was able to pray. God and I were on speaking terms again, and I could trust Him to show mercy to me and my family.

—Marilyn Willett Heavilin

Take Care Of Yourself God!

My daughter Stephanie has always been a very loving, caring child. She started out her prayers that night with the usual, "Dear God, help me not to have nightmares, and please, let it be nice tomorrow." She was ready to close when she said very thoughtfully, ". . . and dear God, please take care of yourself. You are always doing so much for other people. Take some time out and do something special for yourself. Rest up a bit. Amen."

She looked up at me, an angelic smile on her face, then scrambled to scoot under the blankets. I am sure that God felt the same warm loving sensation that I experienced looking down into her smiling face.

—Penny Shoup

13

Spiritual Life

As the deer pants for the water brooks, So my soul pants for Thee, O God.

Psalm 42:1

Evergreen

From Psalm 1:1-3

O Lord, I'd bear some fruit for Thee
If I could just stand still
And let my roots grow deep and wide
Entwined around Thy will.
I'd need to learn to wait for Thee,
To whisper in my heart;
I'd have to let the holy Ghost
Have all, not just a part.

The problem, Lord, I have is this,
I cannot stand quite still;
Too many other neat tree friends
Are planted on my hill.
I feel a little guilty
But I've only me to thank;
I'm far too busy rushing
Up and down my river bank.

There's Myrtle, Rose, and Holly
Who are friends of mine, you know;
We're so busy having fellowship,
We have no time to grow.
They're the cutest little saplings,
The sweetest things to nurse,
There's little time to meditate
On chapter and a verse.

Now I've grown to be an expert
On blight and stunted trees,
So I run extensive seminars

With spiritual expertise.
I tell willows not to wallow
And chestnuts not to crack,
So I'm far too tired to watch and pray
By the time that I get back.

O Lord, don't chop me down and use my trunk for firewood;
I'd love to stop my frantic pace and settle, if I could.
Take hold my tree and planteth me; Don't let my green leaves wither.
Oh, let my thirsty branches drink cool water from thy river.

Dear King of forest glades and glen, O tree King, I adore Thee;
I'll take root where I am planted, content to bring Thee glory.
O spirit, cause my leaves to shine, true fruit at last be seen,
I yield to Thee . . . Oh, touch my tree and keep me evergreen.

—**Jill Briscoe**

Free Gift . . . Free Gift

She wore black to mourn her mother's death. She was a school teacher and part of the group I was speaking to in Rostov-on-Don, Russia. Her sad, wistful, intelligent persona drew my heart to hers in a special way.

We were in Russia at the request of the Minister of Education to teach a curriculum of Judeo-Christian Ethics and Values to school teachers and administrators. Speaking through my translator, Jane, I had referred several times to the free gifts given to us. Free gifts that life gives us, free gifts that God gives us. Her skepticism and resignation to the life and system she had been emersed in was evident by her body language.

"I don't understand, free gift, I don't understand free gift . . . " she repeated several times.

We had chosen to wear very basic clothing and no jewelry on this privileged journey. Respecting the basic lifestyle these people lived and the poverty they experienced was a stark contrast to the abundance of America. However, at the last minute while I was packing I had decided to wear a costume ring which I had loved. As I slipped it on my finger I prayed that God would show me who to give it to.

At the end of our Thursday afternoon session, Vera, my friend in black, stayed to talk further with me. Her questions were profound, her face poignant with the stress and trauma of her personal and country's journey. Again she said, "I don't understand . . . free gift!"

A voice seemed to be saying to me, "Give her the ring." Noticing her stocky fingers I talked back . . . "It won't fit" . . . said good-bye and walked through the long hall, down the stairs and out of The Palace past Lenin's statue to our waiting bus. As I boarded the bus the voice became demanding, "I said, give her the ring!" "O.K., O.K." I felt myself grow in frustration at this unrelenting message and ran back into the place of Lenin's imitation and now our place of teaching. Up the stairs, through the long hall and into the ballroom.

Vera and the translator were still sitting alone in the room. As I quickly pulled the ring from my finger I watched the tears of unbelief fill her eyes. Placing the ring on her little finger I smiled, hugged her and said, "Free gift."

Friday was our last day with these wonderful new friends. They came with arms full of peonies, lilacs and roses. They sang and danced for us in gratefulness for friendship, sharing and the curriculum we had presented.

Vera was the last to leave the room and shyly approached me with something for me. It was a beautiful four-colored book, written in English, of art work through the ages. Knowing the salary of school teachers and the price in Russia, the book probably represented a major portion of a month's earnings. With love, pride and friendship and in English she said, "Now I understand . . . free gift . . . free gift."

And tears sprang to my eyes.

—Naomi Rhode

False Confessions

Confession is very important, but we must be careful to confess only our own mistakes.

After I had talked with a dear friend of mine about the importance of confession, she said to me, "Well, I tried that, Hannah, and it only made the situation worse."

"What did you confess?" I asked.

"I went to somebody and said, 'I forgive you for being so horrible to me. I confess that I have just loathed you for the things you have done'."

She didn't see that her confession was really a judgment of the other person.

—Hannah Hurnard

Held By The Shepherd

The sunlight from outside poured through the church's stained glass windows. Each one depicted a moment in the life of Jesus. As a child, they caught my interest deeply. My father used to drop me off at the church on Sunday mornings on his way to work, and pick me up on his way home. I would sit alone in the church balcony, listening to sermons that made little sense to me, and focusing my attention on the windows.

Finally the organ would begin to play, signaling the end of the service. After the crowd disappeared, I would make my way toward my favorite stained glass window. A small pew was nestled beneath it, and I would crawl up on it to get closer to the beautiful artwork depicting Jesus standing in a field, surrounded by sheep.

One Sunday morning I was feeling especially needy emotionally. Gently I reached upward to touch the feet of Jesus. The glass felt smooth and warm. My eyes met His in a moment of unspoken pain and loneliness. I desperately wanted to be in His arms there among the field of sheep; and for a moment, I could feel myself there, nestled close to His shoulder, wrapped in the warmth of His love.

Then I realized my father would soon be arriving to take me home. Climbing down from the pew, I ran from the sanctuary, across the grassy courtyard, and through the ornate black iron gates. I barely noticed the cold of the tile as I slid up onto the bench, my insides still warmed by the moment before the window in the sanctuary.

For years, as I looked back on that moment in my life, I would always see in my mind Jesus standing among those sheep in the field with a child in His arms. Every detail of the window seemed to have etched itself within my memory through the simplicity of that five-year-old child who beheld it.

A few years later my family moved away; but I carried the memory of that window with me through the years which brought several moves from state to state. Eventually, circumstances returned my family to the area.

Nearly thirty years later, I returned to the church with a friend. I had shared with her my experience before the window, and how the memory of seeing Jesus standing in the field, surrounded by a flock of sheep and holding a child in His arms, carried me through many trials.

I felt a strange warmth inside of me on that cool December day as we slipped through the church doors. It was a weekday and no one was nearer than the church office. As my trembling hands tugged on the heavy wooden doors, I marveled that I was able to slip through them so easily as a child.

Quietly my friend and I entered the sanctuary. The December sun filtered gently through the stained glass windows, lighting the quiet sanctuary with shafts of color that danced on the pews much like I had remembered. My eyes traveled slowly from window to window, taking in their timeless beauty as if it were the first time I had seen them; yet, realizing their familiarity—saving the window which I sought to be viewed last.

My heart seemed to jump into my throat when my eyes finally rested upon the treasured window. There He stood as He did thirty years before, in the center of a meadow with sheep resting at His feet. I felt a bit startled when my gaze rested upon His arms. Where I had remembered there being a child nestled close to His shoulder, there was, instead, a lamb. As I shared the discovery with my friend, she said, "You placed yourself in His arms at that moment as a child, and that image carried you through." It was then that I realized it was I who had been held by the Shepherd all those years.

—Christi Anne Sheppeard

"Are We There Yet?"

When I was little, I'd love it when the whole family would pile into the station wagon and head off to Uncle Doug and Aunt Fran's dairy farm up in northeast Maryland.

All of us kids loved Uncle Doug. He let us milk the cows and feed them grain. It was so much fun to reach out and pet the soft, wet muzzle of a cow munching away on her cud. The barn brimmed with hay where we could build forts and throw straw. And out in the back acres it was "Tomato Wars" with big, juicy, overripe tomatoes.

We'd be in trouble, of course, when we'd come into the farmhouse for dinner, all covered with tomato. But it was all part of the fun.

It really wasn't that far to Uncle Doug's in the car-maybe only fifty miles. But for some reason the trip seemed to take *forever.* Not more than fifteen minutes into the drive we would lean over the front seat and whine, "Are we there yet? When are we gonna get there?" and "Why is it taking so long?"

That memory came back to me recently when I was studying the book of Numbers in the Bible. Freshly released from four centuries of slavery in Egypt, the Israelites were filled with visions of the Promised Land. What a home it would be! Freedom . . . elbow room . . . and what was it God had said? A land "flowing with milk and honey?" It sounded too good to be true.

Thoughts of that beautiful country to the north must have filled their imaginations those first mornings as they would break camp, pack up, and wait for the trumpet to signal another day's march. But just three days into the journey, the Bible tells us they began to murmur and complain.

I can picture them saying to Moses and Aaron, "Are we there yet? When are we going to get there? Why is it taking so long?"

They must have made the trip miserable for Moses, who knew they had quite a long way to go. And much like us kids when we were little, they lacked patience and self-control. They despised the long wait and the boredom of plodding along at what they felt was a very slow pace.

Could it be the same for you and me when we think about heaven, our Promised Land? Does the bright picture of our future Home make us bored and unsatisfied with our lot down here on earth? Do we impatiently think to ourselves, *When are we ever going to get there? Why is it taking so long?* In our lack of perseverance and discipline, do we complain about what seems to be a long wait?

Let's not be like spoiled children. And let's certainly not be like those grumblers in the desert who brought distress to their leaders and grief and anger to their God.

No, the very idea of a Promised Land to come, of heaven yet to be, should fill our hearts with joy and inspire us onward in the journey with strength and real patience.

Are we there yet?

No, not yet. Not quite. But every day brings us closer.

When are we going to get there?

In His time. At the best time. Perhaps sooner than we expect.

Why is it taking so long?

Our loving God must want us Home more than we want to be Home. Yet there is work to do, people to reach, and a Savior to follow down the winding road of days and years.

When we finally turn into heaven's driveway and see Him waiting at the open door, the long drive won't seem so long after all.

—**Joni Eareckson Tada**

And God Said No

I asked God to take away my pride and God said, "No."
He said it was not for Him to take away, but for me to give up.

I asked God to make my handicapped child whole,
And God said, "No."
He said her spirit is whole, her body is only temporary.

I asked God to grant me patience,
And God said, "No."
He said that patience is a byproduct of tribulation,
it isn't granted, it's earned.

I asked God to give me happiness,
And God said, "No."
He said He gives blessings, happiness is up to me.

I asked God to spare me pain,
And God said, "No."
He said, "Suffering draws you apart from worldly cares
and brings you closer to Me."

I asked God to make my spirit grow,
And God said, "No."
He said I must grow on my own, but He will prune me to make me fruitful.

I asked God to help me love others as much as He loves me,
And God said, "Ah, finally you have the idea."

—**Unknown**

I Needed The Quiet

I needed the quiet so He drew me aside.
Into the shadows where we could confide.
Away from the bustle where all the day long
I hurried and worried when active and strong.

I needed the quiet tho at first I rebelled
But gently, so gently, my cross He upheld
And whispered so sweetly of spiritual things
Tho weakened in body, my spirit took wings
To heights never dreamed of when active and gay,
He loved me so greatly He drew me away.

I needed the quiet. No prison my bed,
But a beautiful valley of blessings instead—
A place to grow richer in Jesus to hide.
I needed the quiet so He drew me aside.

—**Alice Hansche Mortenson**

Forgiveness Is Like Tea In A River

God was blessing the retreat where I was speaking. The conference center was set high in the mountains and we enjoyed the sound of a creek swishing outside our meeting room. I had vulnerably shared at the Friday evening session how God delivered me from being a child abuser. Then on Saturday morning, I'd taught on Biblical principles for developing godly self-esteem.

Now it was Saturday afternoon's free time, and I was enjoying visiting privately with many of the women. One woman, Carrie (not her real name), came into my room looking sheepish. After this attractive thirties-something woman sat down and I asked what was on her heart, she hesitantly began, "When I heard you share about being a child abuser, I knew you were the one I could talk to."

She looked down and her face turned pale. I waited. "I've done something as bad as that and I haven't been able to tell anyone. But when I heard you, I figured you were the one." She glanced up at me quickly and then again averted her eyes.

Taking a deep breath, she whispered, "I had an affair with my husband's best friend . . ." After pausing, she rushed on, "He's forgiven me but I can't seem to forgive myself. I keep asking God to forgive me. I tell him over and over again, 'I'm sorry . . .' but I never feel forgiven."

I expressed my appreciation for her sharing with me and we talked for a few minutes about forgiveness being a decision, not a feeling. Soon, it was as if a burden had been removed from her shoulders. She could look me straight in the eye and sat up taller. Confessing her sin to someone else seemed to relieve her of her pain.

We prayed together and I took her through a process of asking God to forgive her and forgiving herself. I sensed God was working an incredible healing in her heart.

When the next woman knocked at my door to indicate Carrie's time had finished, Carrie gave me a quick hug, snatched up her Bible and cup of tea, and hurried out the door . . . smiling.

Later, after the evening session, she came over to me and thrust a piece of lined paper into my hand. "Thanks!" she whispered.

Later in my room, I read what Carrie had written. "Kathy, after speaking with you, I went down to the river to pray. I told God that for the last time I was going to ask for His forgiveness, and then *let it go*. I told Him I was sorry, and to please give me spiritual warfare when the enemy comes.

"Then I did a sort of ceremony. I took the cup of tea I was drinking and said, 'Jesus, this tea represents my sin and this river represents you.' Then I threw the rest of my tea into the river. And you know what I noticed? The tea was immediately washed away! There wasn't a trace of it anywhere! Isn't Jesus wonderful?

"Thank you for introducing me to Him—again."

I was thrilled to read about Carrie's new-found freedom from guilt.

The next morning as we prepared for our final session, Carrie came up to me. I thanked her for the note and she exclaimed, "Kathy, I went back to that same place in the river this morning and guess what? I still couldn't see the tea! It's still gone!"

She gave me another hug, brushed tears from her eyes and turned to find her seat.

I stood there thinking. "Isn't that just like God's forgiveness? It's like sin dropped into the river of God's grace."

—Kathy Collard Miller

Jesus Loves Me

"Jesus loves me, this I know, for the Bible tells me so . . ." This is probably the first song our children learn. It has become so commonplace to us within the church that perhaps we sing it without even thinking about the words.

Try to imagine for a moment what this song might mean if you were hearing it for the very first time.

Jesus? Who is Jesus?

He's the Son of God, the Creator of all things, the King of kings, the Lord of the universe, the sustainer of life.

If he is all that, why does he love me?

Because he created you for fellowship with himself, because he really knows you as a person, because you are important to him as an individual.

Aw, come on, I don't believe it.

It's true—the Bible says so.

The Bible is an old book.

The Bible is the Word of God. His Word will never pass away. It's as relevant today as when it was written, and it says he loves me. "Jesus loves me . . . the Bible tells me so."

A great theologian, known worldwide for his in-depth study of the Scriptures, was asked one day by one of his students, "What is the greatest discovery you have ever made in your extensive searching?"

He answered, "Jesus loves me, this I know, for the Bible tells me so."

This is not a trite saying. It is not a little ditty that sounds cute on the lips of our lisping babies. It is a truth. It is a fact. One we can stake our lives on.

We must never let the little song's familiarity take away from its glorious truth. I will not soon forget the experience I had a few years ago when listening to an excited new Christian who had just discovered something worth shouting about in the

Scriptures. He had found a verse, and he wanted to share it with all of us because it was so special. He could hardly read it for his emotion—it was so new, so exciting, so great a discovery!

His excitement was contagious. We could hardly wait to hear what he had found. He lifted his Bible and, with a quiver in his voice, began to read: *For God so loved the world that he gave his one and only Son, that whoever believes in him shall not perish but have eternal life (John 3:16).*

I settled back in my seat thinking, "Oh, that." I had learned the verse as a child, had heard it repeated often, and had taught it to my own children and to other boys and girls in Sunday school. I had forgotten to be excited about it. I had forgotten what a fantastic discovery it is for someone who has not known it before.

"God so loved the world that he gave his one and only Son . . ." As I watched the face of the new believer, I began to catch the excitement of that verse again. Thank God he loved us! Thank God he loved us so much he sent his Son to free us from our sin. Thank God we can be forgiven, released, made whole because God loved us enough to pay the ultimate price to redeem us.

How wonderful it is to know that Jesus loves me, Jesus loves you. It's true—the Bible tells us so, over and over and over again.

—Janette Oke

Sweet Forgiveness

Family gatherings were common during my childhood days on the farm, but I remember in particular one potluck picnic in our big front yard. When it was time to eat, aunts and uncles and older cousins all gathered around as the fried chicken, baked ham, and casseroles were brought out from the kitchen. I barely nibbled at my potato salad and ham. I was leaving room for the desserts that were still sitting on the counter in the back kitchen. I wondered what lay under those checkered tea towels? Molasses cookies? Chocolate cake? Date squares?

While the adults were still busily engaged in conversation and second helpings, I sneaked in to take a look. Gingerly lifting up the corner of each towel, I saw tarts, cookies, squares, and pies; but one cake in particular caught my attention.

At five years of age I had already grown wise as to what happens to certain inferior cakes that fall slightly in the middle. More than once I had watched my distraught mother as she tried to cover the evidence with icing. I now saw that the cake under Aunt Dorothy's tea towel had a slightly concave surface, and I knew that the fudge icing would be thickest at the center.

I peeked outside. Everyone was still lingering over the main course. Why did they have to take so long to get to the dessert?

Not willing to wait any longer, I finally took a table knife from the cutlery drawer and cut a nice *big* piece of cake for myself right from the center where the icing was thickest. And then I sneaked upstairs to eat it.

I had no sooner finished the last bite than my mother and Aunt Dorothy came into the kitchen to get the desserts. I held my breath as I stood at the top of the stairway, listening.

After what seemed an eternity, Aunt Dorothy lifted the tea towel from her cake and exclaimed, "Well, well, Rose, there must be a mouse in your house. Just look at this!"

Fully expecting a sharp reprimand, I waited. And waited.

But for some strange reason, the women seemed far more concerned about how they would cut the pies, and when the screen door banged shut behind them, I knew I was safe, but too embarrassed to show my face for the rest of the day.

That night when I said my prayers, I silently asked God to forgive me for stealing the piece of cake with the thickest icing; but I still felt guilty about it. Aunt Dorothy never ever mentioned the episode again. Had she already forgiven me? I very much doubted it.

And then I got the chance to ask her directly.

It was at another family gathering, only by this time the years had slipped away and my aunts and uncles were all white-haired guests. I was now the one overseeing the desserts, so I decided to select a certain piece of cake just for Aunt Dorothy.

"But my dear, you didn't have to bring me the piece with the most icing on it," she protested.

"That's to make up for the piece I stole 45 years ago," I said. "Can you forgive me?"

"Forgive you? I can't even remember it," she exclaimed, and her brown eyes twinkled with amusement. "Tell me about it."

Try as she might, she could not recall the incident.

"Mercy! I never did bake the lightest cakes; but that piece must have been especially heavy if it weighed on your conscience like that. I'm sure I forgave you the day it happened, otherwise I would remember it. But to think it bothered you all that time . . ."

Later, it crossed my mind that in forgiving us our sins, God is like Aunt Dorothy. He promptly forgets. And when Aunt Dorothy forgives, she's like God. I had to smile at the strong family resemblance.

—Alma Barkman

Road Blocks And Rubber Bands

Huffing and puffing in the early morning sun, my girlfriend and I ran behind the Laundromat and donut shop with its aromas beckoning us to stop our three-mile run. Soon we'd passed the fire station, and up ahead on the right a little boy around five years old stood grinning in his striped T-shirt and baggy shorts. Next to him was the sweetest looking little girl wearing a pink quilted robe and slippers, clutching a small doll.

"Are you firemens?" the boy asked, still smiling brightly.

For a moment I puffed up thinking he had mistaken us for one of the fire crew. I now knew all the hard work we'd put in was finally paying off.

"No. We're not," I answered, still glowing from the mistaken identity.

"Good!" he said. "Now I'm gonna' hit you with a rubber band!" He ran after us aiming at our backsides with the largest rubber bands I'd ever seen.

"Ha! Ha! I got the one in the white shorts!" He ran laughing back to his hideout as the little girl swooned over his bravery.

On our return trip, we could see their legs under the van as they prepared to attack again.

I whispered to my friend, Paula, "Let me handle this."

We continued on when the boy rushed out to attack us. I turned to confront the pair. "Does your Mom know you shoot people with rubber bands?" I asked, sweat dripping off my nose as I towered over the four foot monster.

"Yes!" he answered defiantly.

"Okay, let's go ask her right now if she allows you to do that." I reached for his hand to take him to the front door.

His eyes got as large as saucers when the little girl spoke up in his defense, "His mother isn't here."

"Fine," I said, still heading for the door. "I'll ask whoever is home."

All of a sudden the little giant shrank in bravery and screamed to his cohort, "Run!"

We turned to continue our run when he suddenly attacked from the rear again.

"I'm gonna get you now," he yelled, running towards us.

I stopped cold and faced him. Each step I took towards him, the more he shrank in courage. "Come on, let's go to the door right now and ring the bell together."

"No, no, no!" he begged.

"Do you promise to never hit people passing by with rubber bands?" I asked him with a stern face.

"Yyess . . ." he muttered, eyes darting anywhere to avoid my direct stare.

"What's your name?" I asked.

"Greg," he said meekly, eyes downcast.

"Greg, now that I know your name and you've made a promise to not hit people with rubber bands, you must remain a man of your word. Do you understand?"

"Yes," he answered with a voice more like a mouse than the ferocious lion that had just breathed down our necks.

We turned confidently this time to continue our run, never looking back because we could hear them retreating in the opposite direction.

Later in the day the Lord reminded me that the devil is much like that little boy: brave behind my back, lying to my face and returning to attack when I think I'm safe. More importantly, Satan's just a squirt when I stand my ground and remind him that God's Word is able to reduce him to his proper size.

—**Lille Diane**

Through The Eyes Of Love

As the UPS truck rattled into the driveway, I heaved a happy sigh of relief, knowing the last of the Christmas presents I'd ordered had finally arrived. I had finished my shopping—a month early!

"Hi," the young man said as he handed me the package. As I took it from him I noticed a bit of drab brown cloth protruding from a tiny hole.

"Oh, dear," I thought as I took it from him. "I sure don't like the color of that dress; I hope both aren't alike. I wanted at least one of the girls' dolls to have a bright cheerful look."

I tore at the package, and out tumbled two of the ugliest dolls I'd ever seen in my life. *Well, that's what you get for ordering from a magazine,* I mentally scolded myself, holding them up for a closer look.

Their hair looked like someone had dredged it out of the ocean. One eye looked at me, while the other stared blankly into space. One's mouth was tiny and pursed, and the other's was rather large and sneering; one cheek bright, one cheek pale; one hand well-formed, the other . . . *Oh, what a rip-off!* I stuffed them into my closet. *I'll not even give them to Dawn and Tammy for Christmas. I'd just be embarrassed at their looks of disappointment.*

With the bustle of Thanksgiving, cookies and fun, I soon forgot all about the two little dolls I had shoved out of sight in the bedroom closet.

The girls were home from school for Thanksgiving vacation and busy with the usual make-believe games in their rooms. They decided to play dress-up. Off they scurried to Mom's closet for some "grown-up" clothes.

I was at the sink finishing the breakfast dishes when I heard both girls squeal with delight.

"Mommy, Mommy," Dawn screamed, "She's beautiful! Can I have her?"

I heard their feet thundering down the hall and turned to see two happy little girls with glowing faces, tenderly cradling those ugly dolls in their arms.

"Are they for us?" Tammy asked anxiously, her eyes sparkling.

"Oh, I hope so!" Dawn echoed.

"I'm naming mine Cathy," Tammy said, proudly hugging the doll more closely to her.

"And I'll call mine Candy," Dawn announced boldly. "Oh, Mom, please say they're ours."

"Yes, girls, they are for you. I'm so glad you like them," I said in disbelief.

"Like them . . . we love them!" they both chimed excitedly, as each gave me a happy hug.

"Thanks, Mom," they called over their shoulders as they disappeared to play with their new-found friends.

Their cheerful voices faded as my busy mind returned to the day of the dolls' arrival. I recalled the many flaws I had noticed immediately. How ugly they seemed to me, how drab—and that hair! But Dawn and Tammy hadn't noticed the faults at all, because they weren't looking for any. They saw these dolls through different eyes. Where I saw flaws, they saw perfection; where I saw nothing of value, they found something to prize.

How often we seem only to notice a much-too-large nose or eyes that seem dull, unruly hair, or lack of quick wit and various other talents of ourselves or those around us. We often maximize the flaws and minimize the assets. Yet in the eyes of God, we are as those dolls were to my girls . . . beautiful and complete.

—**Marcia Krugh Leaser**

Lord, Please Meet Me In The Laundry Room

I was a new Christian nine years ago when I first heard the term "prayer closet," and began to feel inadequate. Someone might say something like, "She fled to her prayer closet and poured her heart out to the Lord." I also deserved a prayer closet to flee to. So I would hurry home to look for any previously uncharted territory to call my own. But with the hordes in my house, I could find nowhere with the sustained privacy necessary for even a prayer shoebox.

One day, as I was unrolling a multitude of balled-up socks for the washer, I prayed, "Lord, is there a prayer closet somewhere for me? And what about this thing they call 'quiet time'?"

"Aren't you praying now?" This question was wordlessly impressed upon my heart.

"Yes, but Lord . . ." and things began to spill out of my heart that I hardly knew were there. I didn't have to tell Him how hard it was to feel like a lightweight when others had more spiritual muscle to flex. I didn't have to tell Him how much I wanted to be the best I could be, and how far from the best I often felt. I didn't have to tell Him because He already knew. But since He was listening, I told Him anyway.

Somehow I was made to understand that a mother of toddlers isn't like anyone else. I felt comforted; I felt loved; I felt like He cared for me just as I was. Maybe I cried a little. Probably I laughed as well. I did a lot of praying and a lot of laundry before we were through.

And so my laundry room became my prayer closet. This is where I meet the Lord each morning before my children awake, and at intervals throughout the day as I transfer clothes from baskets to washer, from washer to dryer, from dryer to baskets again. In these twelve and twenty minute snatches, I have found my quiet time.

My four-year-old son, Jonathan, spent his first two years in and out of the hospital. My laundry room, with its reassuring routine and memories of mornings with God, became the most comfortable place for me when I could not be at my son's side. People must have questioned my sanity when I staggered home from the hospital and made a beeline for the laundry room. How could I explain what it had become?

Many prayers and loads of laundry later, I now wonder if there are other mothers like me—mothers too busy wiping peanut butter and jelly off little faces and kissing boo-boos to maintain the practice of what the less encumbered call "quiet time."

Are there mommies whose prayer closets are buckets and scrub brushes, sewing baskets, garden patches, or car pools? Are there mommies whose prayer closets are assembly lines or switchboards or operating rooms? Are there mommies squeezing moments of quiet time between customer calls or the clamor of kids?

I wonder—because now I understand that God is bigger than any place I set aside to meet Him, and as near as I invite Him to be.

—Barbara Curtis

God Works A Miracle

When my third child was born with a severe birth defect my stamina was challenged as never before! Brian had to wear full leg casts from the day of birth until he was over a year old. He was naturally a light and restless sleeper and the casts further complicated the situation.

Whenever he tried to turn over or change position, the weight of the casts would awaken him. He rarely slept for more than twenty to thirty minutes at a time. When thus awakened he would cry, thereby waking me, too. So neither of us ever got enough sleep.

As the months went by I became progressively more exhausted. The more tired I became, the more depressed I felt. I could not nap during the day because the other two boys required my supervision even if the baby fell asleep.

I stopped trying to go to church. Getting myself and three little ones ready proved too great a challenge for my diminished energies. But I did maintain daily devotions.

One morning my scripture reading was Isaiah 40:29-31. "He gives power to the tired and worn out, and strength to the weak. Even the youths will be exhausted. But they who wait upon the Lord shall renew their strength. They shall mount up with wings like eagles; they shall run and not be weary; they shall walk and not faint."

These verses leaped off the page at me. But what did it mean to "Wait upon the Lord?" I pondered this all day long.

Late that afternoon my mother called to ask if I was planning on cooking Thanksgiving dinner that year. It was my turn. I told her we were canceling Thanksgiving because I was too tired to even eat it, much less cook it! The holiday was thirty-two days away. She said she would be glad to have it if I still didn't feel up to it in November.

That evening I re-read Isaiah 40:31. I still didn't understand exactly how one "waited upon the Lord," but I decided I was going to try it to see if God would restore my strength.

I resolved to spend one hour every morning just waiting on God. To do this I had to get up at 5:45 a.m. Of course it made no sense to get up an hour earlier when what I suffered from was too little sleep! But I was desperate enough to try it. I vowed to continue this "waiting" for thirty days. If my vitality didn't increase I would give it up.

So the next morning I rose at 5:45 and put Brian in our bed, telling my husband he was on duty for the next sixty minutes.

Our living room had a huge picture window on the east wall. With Bible in hand I sat on the stair landing and looked out that window at the still dark, sleeping world. As I watched I recited Psalms 100 and 103, then the critical passage in Isaiah. I asked God to come into my life in such a powerful way that my strength "would be renewed like the eagles," so I, too, could "run and not be weary, walk and not faint."

That first morning nothing unusual happened; but I *did* enjoy the peace and quiet of an hour alone with God. It was beautifully still-until the sun came up and summoned the birds from their slumber. As I watched and listened, it was as though the birds were singing, "Morning has broken." I decided to keep my appointment with God the next day, too, just for the sheer enjoyment of the stillness and the dawn's beauty.

For twenty-nine consecutive mornings I sat and greeted God and the new day. It was pleasant, but I grew progressively more exhausted. I was relieved as I struggled out of bed at 5:45 on the thirtieth day for what was, I thought, the last time.

But this morning proved to be very different from the previous twenty-nine. I sat as usual, praying and praising God, watching the horizon brighten. As the rim of the sun appeared I began to feel a warmth throughout my entire body. Simultaneously I was filled with joy! An elation like nothing I had ever experienced overwhelmed me, and suddenly I was bursting with energy!

This strength never abated. I called my mother that day and told her I would cook Thanksgiving dinner, after all. At the end of the day I was still going strong.

Brian continued to be a restless sleeper and I unfailingly rose an hour early to wait upon the Lord for several more months. But eventually his problems were corrected, the casts removed, and he began to sleep more normally. As long as I arose and spent that first hour with God my energy seemed inexhaustible. When I stopped getting up at 5:45 my energy slowly dwindled. Recognizing what had happened, I reestablished that precious hour. I still spend the first hour of the day waiting upon the King of Glory. He never disappoints me! He is always there—waiting for me.

—**Nancy L. Dorner**

He Is The Bridegroom

Flying home from Atlanta one Saturday evening, I sat next to a young woman who was impeccably groomed in every way, except for the streaks on her cheeks where tears had removed some of her soft red blush.

My heart went out to her, but my head said, *None of your business, Liz, Don't interfere.*

As usual, I ignored my head and went with my heart. "What brings you to Louisville?" I asked softly.

She turned my direction, and a fresh flow of tears began as she moaned, "I don't know!"

Inside, a still, small voice said, *Hush . . . let her talk!* So I pressed my lips together (for me, that's almost an aerobic exercise), assumed my most compassionate expression, and nodded.

"I'm g-g-getting married," she stammered, daintily blowing her perfectly powdered nose.

"How wonderful!" I exclaimed, despite my vow of silence.

"I'm not so sure," she said, her voice still shaking. "My entire family and all my friends live in Florida, plus I have a great job there. I'm leaving my whole life behind." Another trickle of tears slipped out of the corner of her eye.

"I moved to Louisville from far away too," I said, trying to encourage her. "It's a great place to live."

"I guess so," she said, sounding unconvinced.

Despite my efforts, I was not helping one bit. Then, the perfect question suddenly presented itself: "Do you love him?"

Her expression changed instantly. "Oh, yes!" she said, then blushed at her own enthusiasm. "He's very kind and considerate, really intelligent, and handsome too." As she brushed away the last of her tears, she told me all about her beloved fiancé, how much fun they had together, how impressed her family was with him, and yes, how much she loved him. I smiled, nodded, and listened, knowing no further questions would be needed.

When we landed and headed into the gate area, I picked him out of the crowd instantly. Even from a distance, he was obviously a fine young man. Tall, strong, yet with a warm and gentle smile and armed with a dozen red roses that matched her red suit perfectly. When she ran into his arms with a teary smile, I made myself look away (very difficult!) rather than invade their privacy but found a few happy tears had sneaked into my own eyes.

The truth is, when you find the right One, it's easy to forsake all others and follow him.

—Liz Curtis Higgs

DESTINATION UNKNOWN

ONE morning, my four-year old son, Kevin, and his grandpa went out to buy donuts. On the way, grandpa turned to Kevin and asked "Which way is heaven?" Kevin pointed to the sky. "Which way is hell?" Kevin pointed towards the floor of the truck. Grandpa continued, were are we going?" Dunkin' Donuts," Kevin replied.

—Kathy Chapman

Earthquake

My family had gathered at my house for our yearly family reunion. We all went to church together and while we were singing the opening hymn, an earthquake hit. The building shook, and the overhead lights began to swing back and forth. In true California style, we never missed a beat, even though we had to grab the pew in front to steady ourselves.

Following the service, the pastor came over to greet my out-of-town relatives. My son-in-law grinned impishly as he shook the pastor's hand and said, "I've been to many church services in my life, but I can honestly say this was the most moving one I've ever attended."

We all had to agree!

—June Cerza Kolf

Credits

Just Passing Through from *Abiding in Christ*, Cynthia Heald, Nav Press, Colorado, 1996. Used by permission.

About Your Timing, Lord . . . from *Startled by Silence,* Ruth Senter, Zondervan/Daybreak, Michigan, 1986. Used by permission.

Jumping Jehosaphat from *Normal Is Just A Setting On Your Dryer*, Patsy Clairmont, Focus on the Family Publishing, Colorado, 1993. Used by permission.

On His Shoulders from *What My Parents Did Right*, compiled and edited by Gloria Gaither, Star Song Publishing Group, Tennessee, 1991. Used by permission.

How to Be a Fun Grandparent from *Parents & Children*, Chariot Victor Publishing, edited by Jay Kesler, Ron Beers, & LaVonne Neff, 1986. Used by permission.

Everyone Needs Someone from *Everyone Needs Someone,* Helen Steiner Rice, Revell, a division of Baker Book House Company, Michigan, 1978. Used by permission.

Unscheduled Flight from *"One Size Fits All" and Other Fables,* Liz Curtis Higgs, Thomas Nelson Publishers, Tennessee, 1993. Used by permission.

Fun Is Where You Find It from *Fresh Elastic for Stretched Out Moms,* Barbara Johnson, Revell, a division of Baker Book House Company, Michigan, 1986. Used by permission.

Letting Go from *A Woman's Guide to Breaking Bondages*, Quinn Sherrer and Ruthanne Garlock, Servant Publications, Michigan, 1994. Used by permission.

She Released Me from *What My Parents Did Right*, compiled and edited by Gloria Gaither, Star Song Publishing Group, Tennessee, 1991. Used by permission.

The Forgiving Formula from *Practical Christianity*, compiled by LaVonne Neff, Ron Beers, Bruce Barton, Linda Taylor, Dave Veerman & Jim Galvin, Tyndale Publishers, Illinois, 1987. Used by permission.

He's No Mind Reader from *Can I Control My Changing Emotions?* Annie Chapman, Luci Shaw and Florence Littauer, Bethany House Publishers, Minnesota, 1994. Used by permission.

Learning To Trust adapted from *Pure Pleasure,* Bill & Pam Farrel and Jim & Sally Conway, IVP, Illinois, 1994. Used by permission.

Be My Friend from *Can I Control My Changing Emotions?* Annie Chapman, Luci Shaw and Florence Littauer, Bethany House Publishers, Minnesota, 1994. Used by permission.

Tribute from *What My Parents Did Right*, compiled and edited by Gloria Gaither, Star Song Publishing Group, Tennessee, 1991. Used by permission.

The Problem from *Weather of the Heart*, Gigi Graham Tchividjian, Multnomah Books, Questar Publishers, Oregon, 1991. Used by permission.

Praying Without Words from *Enjoying the Presence of God,* Jan Johnson, NavPress, Colorado, 1996. Used by permission.

Lessons on Love from *What My Parents Did Right*, compiled and edited by Gloria Gaither, Star Song Publishing Group, Tennessee, 1991. Used by permission.

Pray for Mercy from *When Your Dreams Die*, Marilyn Willett Heavilin, Thomas Nelson, Tennessee, 1995. Used by permission.

False Confessions from *Practical Christianity*, compiled by LaVonne Neff, Ron Beers, Bruce Barton, Linda Taylor, Dave Veerman & Jim Galvin, Tyndale Publishers, Illinois, 1987. Used by permission.

"Are We There Yet?" from *Glorious Intruder*, Joni Eareckson Tada, Multnomah Books, Questar Publishers, Oregon, 1989. Used by permission.

I Needed the Quiet from *I Needed the Quiet*, Alice Hansche Mortenson, Beacon Hill Press, Missouri, 1978. Used by permission.

Jesus Loves Me from *Practical Christianity*, compiled by LaVonne Neff, Ron Beers, Bruce Barton, Linda Taylor, Dave Veerman & Jim Galvin, Tyndale Publishers, Illinois, 1987. Used by permission.

God Works A Miracle from *A Woman's Guide to Spiritual Power*, Nancy L. Dorner, Starburst, 1992. Used by permission.

He is the Bridegroom from *Reflecting His Image*, Liz Curtis Higgs, Thomas Nelson, Tennessee, 1996. Used by permission.

Who's in the Driver's Seat? from *Stories from the Front Lines: Power Evangelism in Today's World,* Jane Rumph, Chosen Books, 1996. Used by permission.

Contributors

Debora Allen, a freelance writer, dreams of moving to Arizona to feel the warmth of the sun, eat fajitas, and write affirming, lyrical fiction under the name Adrienne Allen. She would like to hear from readers, especially Arizona residents. Contact: 36 Clinton Street, Apt. 5, Rensselaer, NY 12144. (518) 434-5829.

Esther M. Bailey devotes her time to freelance writing since retiring from a business career. In addition to more than 600 published credits, she has co-authored a book with Lori Salierno, *Designed for Excellence*. Esther is married to Ray. Contact: 4631 E. Solano Dr., Phoenix, AZ 85018. (602) 840-3143.

Alma Barkman, freelance writer and photographer, is author of six books that combine humor and inspiration. Married for forty years and the mother of four children, she and husband, Leo, live in central Canada, where they enjoy gardening and "do-it-yourself" projects.

Virginia Baty is editorial assistant for the Nazarene World Mission Society and a freelance writer of numerous articles and poems. She is married to Daniel, has five children and 13 great-grandchildren. Contact: 412 Meadowbrook Lane, Olathe, KS 66062.

Georgia Burkett, a freelancer whose devotionals and short stories appear in a wide variety of Christian and historical publications, also teaches a Junior Sunday school class. She enjoys her large family of children, grandchildren, and great-grandchildren. Georgia also does needlework, gardening, and clowning.

Sandy Cathcart, free-lance writer, speaker, musician/singer, and Bible courier, is editor for Wilderness Trails Newsletter (a ministry to troubled youth). She shares a message of encouragement for believers to put feet to their faith. Contact: 341 Flounce Rock Rd., Prospect, OR 97536. (541) 560-2367.

Irene Carloni writes articles, devotionals, and is an editor and producer. She has received awards for work with cable TV. Irene enjoys photography, crafts, and Bible study. The Carlonis have three children. Contact: 6 Cambridge, Manhattan Beach, CA 90266. (310) 546-5547.

Arlene Centerwall is a Canadian nurse recently married for the first time at the age of 55 to an Oregon Physician. She became a Christian 35 years ago and has always felt an inclination to share the wonderful ways of the Lord through the printed word.

Jeri Chrysong has been published in various devotional books, as well as *God's Vitamin "C" for the Spirit* and *God's Vitamin "C" for the Christmas Spirit*. She also writes commentaries and opinions for newspapers, and is a poet. Jeri is a legal secretary and lives with her two sons in Huntington Beach, California.

Mary Cotton is a retired English and Reading teacher. She and husband Seth have six children, four foster children, 15 grandchildren and 5 great-grandchildren. Mary writes articles, stories and poetry and likes to read, swim and bike. Contact: 1060 N. Meadowbrook, White Cloud, MI 49349-9719.

Vanessa Craig studied English literature and art history at the University of California, Irvine. She has worked in the television industry and is currently producing "edutainment" children's programming. Vanessa enjoys writing and painting. She is married to William and has two children.

Doris C. Crandall, an inspirational writer, has been published in *Christian Education Today, Mature Living, Guideposts, Christian Herald* and others. She is co-founder of a read and critique group. Contact: 2303 Victoria, Amarillo, TX 79106. (806) 355-0533.

Anesa Cronin lives in Riverside, California. She has been with San Bernardino County Probation 19 years. Anesa has two Master's Degrees in Correctional Counseling and Counseling Psychology; two credentials in Pupil Personnel and adult education. She taught at Inland Christian Bible College and has traveled extensively.

Barbara Curtis, besides being the mother of eleven, has published in over 40 Christian publications and is the author of *Small Beginnings: First Steps to Prepare Your Toddler for Lifelong Learning*. Contact: 788 Rowland Blvd. Novato, CA 94947. Email: Ajointheir@aol.com.

Lille Diane has inspired thousands nationwide with her personal story and concert, "From Ashes to Beauty." Lille's refreshing speaking style combines humor, music and exhortation in her presentations. Contact: P.O. Box 924, Oak View, CA 93022. (805) 649-1805.

Denise A. DeWald is a writer whose works have appeared in *The Upper Room*, Barbour Books, etc. Some of her poems have been made into songs, one of which has been aired on Family Life Radio. Contact: 1744 Swenson Road, Au Gres, MI 48703 (517) 876-8718.

Nancy L. Dorner is a free-lance speaker, writer, retreat leader and director of Creative Directions, a Christian seminar service. She has written three books: *A Women's Guide to Spiritual Power*, and *Glimpses of Grace and Glory*. Contact: 5030 Angling Rd., Kalamazoo, MI 49008. (616) 344-5852.

Marjorie K. Evans is a freelance writer of many articles and a former teacher. She enjoys grandparenting, reading, church work, traveling, her Welsh Corgi, and tending plants. She and husband, Edgar, have two sons and five grandchildren. Contact: 4162 Fireside Circle, Irvine, CA 92604-2216. (714) 551-5296.

Betty Steele Everett is a wife, mother, and grandmother living in Defiance, Ohio. She has written for Christian publications for 40 years, with six books and more than 4000 shorter items published. Her hobbies are letter writing, speed walking, traveling, and an occasional round of golf. Contact: 2309 Riviera Rd., Defiance, OH 43512-3707.

Florence Ferrier and her husband, Darwin, live near Baudette, in Northern Minnesota. She is a former social worker and now does volunteer work in addition to freelance writing. Her work has appeared in over 40 magazines plus other publications.

Mary Bahr Fritts has authored juvenile titles, *The Memory Box*, *Jordi's Run* and an essay in *Guiltless Catholic Parenting.* Winner of nine writing awards, she has published 125+ stories, columns, reviews and articles. Contact: 807 Hercules Place, Colorado Springs, CO 80906. (719) 630-8244.

Brenda Foltz works at Adventurous Christians, a wilderness camp. She enjoys people, running, skiing, canoeing, calligraphy, guitar, singing, playing Scrabble, doing cartwheels . . . and praises God for ants! Contact: 7910-335th Ave. NW., Princeton, MN 55371. (612) 389-4920.

Nancy L. Goodwin is a freelance writer of both prose and poetry, a wife, and mother of two. She has enough college credits to be educated, not enough to be graduated. Her favorite things are reading and writing (but not arithmetic). (614) 439-3512.

Lynell Gray has been married for 27 years to her college sweetheart, Steve. They have three children. Lynell is a second grade teacher, and author of a chapter in a professional book for educators on the Theory of Multiple Intelligencies. Contact: 2867 Balfore Street, Riverside, CA (909) 788-2638.

Judy Hampton has her own business and is a featured speaker for retreats, conferences and Christian organizations. She is also involved in several outreach ministries. Contact: 670 Oakhaven Ave., Brea, CA 92826. (714) 528-0704.

Judith Hayes has been a professional freelance writer since 1993. She and Michael Hayes have been married for 26 years, and are the proud parents of Sasha (24 years old), and Annabelle (20 years old). She loves to write and share hope and faith. She lives in Chatsworth, CA (818) 701-9775.

Sarah Healton, Ed.D., is retired and has been published in the Anytime Craft Series, skill-building books, co-authored with her daughter, Kay. Her hobbies include reading, writing, sewing and traveling.

Barbara J. Hibschman is a pastor's wife, mother, former missionary to the Philippines, and teacher. She is a speaker, author of 8 books, over 200 articles and poems, and contributing author to 7 devotional books. Contact: 95 Dock Watch Hollow Rd., Warren, NJ 07059. (908) 560-0910.

Irene Horst is a freelance writer from Millersville, PA. Her writings have appeared in numerous Christian and secular publications. For more than 18 years she has been a weekly columnist for the *Tri-County Record* Newspaper.

Melanie Hubbard lives in a small town at the foot of the Sierra Nevada Mountains. She enjoys gardening, sewing, camping and being with her family. Contact: P.O. Box 816, Lone Pine, CA 93545.

Michele T. Huey is a wife and mother of three. She has a teaching degree in English and currently teaches adult education classes part-time, evaluates home-schoolers and writes feature stories for her local newspaper. Her three loves are writing, teaching, and making music. Contact: R.D. 1, Box 112, Glen Campbell, PA 15742. (814) 845-7683.

Bettymae J. Huff writes short devotionals, poems, and true stories. She has been published in *Catholic Digest* and won top prizes in writing contests of the Catholic diocese of Monterey in California. She was published in *God's Vitamin "C" for the Spirit*. She resides in Atascadero, CA (805) 461-5619.

Jan Johnson is a retreat speaker and author of seven books, including *Enjoying the Presence of God*, and hundreds of Bible studies and magazine articles. Contact: 4897 Abilene St., Simi, CA 93063. (805) 522-3221.

Sharon Jones is adept as an author, educator, and conference speaker, passionately encouraging Christian women and youth to live Biblical truth. In addition to her freelance work, she is co-publisher of *Ishshah* magazine and managing editor of *Christteen* magazine. Contact: P.O. Box 1519, Inglewood, CA 90308. (213) 750-7573.

Kathy Keidel lives in a mountain community with her husband and two children, ages 8 and 11. She teaches elementary school and has a Master's Degree in "Creative Arts in Learning." Her hobbies include writing for children. Contact: P.O. Box 938, Buena Vista, CO 81211. (719) 395-8704.

Mary K. Kasting is a freelance writer and artist. She is a Bethel Bible series leader, Caring Evangelism teacher and a Stephen Minister. Together with husband, Art, they co-direct "Lift His Banners High." Contact: 5129 Marble Court, Indianapolis, IN 46237-3023. (317) 784-0314.

Mary Lou Klingler raised four children, is an R.N. and freelance writer. Howard is her husband of 49 years. She founded and co-led a Christian writers' club for 15 years. Contact: 300 North Drive, Paulding, OH 45879-1025. (419) 399-3089 (Summer); 1056 E. Pueblo Rd., Phoenix, AZ 85020-4120 (Winter).

June Cerza Kolf is an inspirational writer and hospice worker. She has published over one hundred articles and five books. She offers grief workshops and training for hospice volunteers. She and her husband live in Quartz Hill, CA.

Marcia Krugh Leaser is a free-lance Christian writer who has been writing for twenty years. Her poems and articles have appeared in magazines like *Ideals, Decision,* and *Standard.* Marcia's song ministry includes her original poems. Contact: 2613 C. R. 118, Fremont, OH 43420. (419) 992-4307.

Georgia Curtis Ling is an entertaining speaker, writer and newspaper columnist who shares about faith, love and life. She is published in numerous magazines, and newspapers. This is her third appearance in a *God's Vitamin "C" for the Spirit* book. Contact: 4716 W. Glenhaven Drive, Everett, WA 98203. (206) 257-0377.

Connie Merritt is an engaging and humorous professional speaker and author of *Finding Love Again: The Dating Survival Manual for Women over Thirty* and *Tame the Lions in Your Life-Dealing with Difficult People and Tough Times.* Contact: P.O. Box 9075, Laguna Beach, CA 92677. (714) 494-0091.

Kathy Collard Miller is the best selling author of the *God's Vitamin "C" for the Spirit* series with her husband, Larry. The author of 25 books, she is also a popular speaker both nationally and internationally. Contact: P.O. Box 1058, Placentia, CA 92871. (714) 993-2654.

Elaine Munyan is a wife and mother of eight. She enjoys reading, writing, cooking and playing the piano. Elaine has homeschooled for seven years and studied music therapy at the University of Kansas. Contact: 9443 Connell Dr., Overland Park, KS 66212. (913) 541-8256.

Deborah Sillas Nell lives with her husband, Craig, and daughter Sophia. Deborah is a stay-at-home mom who writes, paints and enjoys praying for and ministering to those who are hurting emotionally. Contact: 12571 Sunswept Ave. #7, Garden Grove, CA 92843. (714) 265-1364.

Pat Palau and her husband, international evangelist Luis Palau, live in Portland, Oregon. They have extensive speaking and writing ministries, including contributing several chapters to *Keeping Your Kids Christian* and co-authoring the booklet *How to Lead Your Child to Christ.*

Nancy E. Peterson has been a Christian writer and cartoonist for ten years. Her work has appeared in publications including *Housewife-Writer's Forum, The Press Enterprise,* and *the Inland Empire Christian Writer's Guild Newsletter*. She was founding editor of *The Bundy Canyon Christian Church Newsletter*.

Cora Lee Pless, a free-lance writer, has had articles published by numerous periodicals including *Guideposts, Decision,* and *The Christian Reader*. Cora Lee enjoys teaching Sunday School and is available as an inspirational speaker. Contact: 127 Overhead Bridge Rd., Mooresville, NC 28115. (704) 664-5655.

Lois Erisey Poole is married to Robert. She has been writing for 20 years and has been published extensively throughout North America. She has just completed her first book, *Ring Around The Moon*. Contact: P. O. Box 3402, Quartz Hill, CA 93586-0402.

Dr. Kathryn Presley is Associate Professor of English at Lamar University-Port Arthur. Married 43 years to Roy Presley, Kathryn is a former school superintendent, mother of two and grandmother of four. She speaks and has published poetry, essays and short stories.

Christie Qualls is a popular retreat speaker and Bible study leader. She speaks on personal vision, evangelism, eating disorders, bridal love for Christ, and singleness as well as other subjects. She is also an accomplished artist. Contact: 78 N. Understory Ln., Tucson, AZ 85748. (520) 722-9273.

Shirley A. Reynolds is a housewife, freelance writer, mother of one daughter and has been married 31 years. She works with street youth and a food bank, and sings in her local church choir. Shirley has been blessed to experience God's miracles and hopes to serve Him through writing.

Naomi Rhode, RDH, CPAE, is past president of the National Speakers Association. In her inspirational, dynamic speaking, she shares on team building, interpersonal communication and motivation. Naomi has authored *The Gift of Family* and *More Beautiful Than Diamonds—The Gift of Friendship*.

Karen Robertson is a teacher, freelance writer, and inspirational speaker. A recent graduate of Clown school, Karen sometimes appears as Ditzi the Clown. Contact: 33140 Claremont Street, Wildomar, CA 92595. (909) 678-3030.

Therese A. Robertson is an aspiring young writer and office administrator for the church she attends in San Francisco. A wife and mother of two young children, she still makes time to lead group Bible studies and speak at women's functions. Contact: 397 Shipley Ave., Daly City, CA 94015-2826.

Jean Rodgers is a self-employed writer of promotional pieces and wrote a newspaper column, "We Women," for ten years. She has dozens of published essays and is the mother of four and grandmother of six. Contact: 2350 South 25th Ave., Broadview, IL 60153-3800. (708) 681-4294.

Gail Ronveaux is a pastor's wife, coordinator of M.O.P.S., mother of three children and the Director of Graduate Programs at California Baptist College in Riverside. Contact: 5320 Victoria Ave., Riverside, CA 92506. (909) 683-3955.

Jane Rumph is a free-lance editor and author of *Stories from the Front Lines*. An honors graduate of Occidental College, she serves on the board of directors of Global Harvest Ministries. As a writer and intercessor, she has traveled to 20 countries on five continents.

Nancy I. Sanders enjoys painting scenic nature spots with her husband Jeff and sons Dan and Ben. Her most recent children's books include the *Marshal Matt Mysteries with a Value* series for beginning readers. Contact: 15212 Mariposa Ave., Chino Hills, CA 91709.

Marilyn Gross Scogin teaches special education, writes, and is an avid guitar player. She is a wife, mother, and grandmother. Marilyn and her husband, Harold, teach Bible classes in their home and at church. Contact: 16109 Jersey Dr., Houston, TX 77040. (713) 466-6598.

Christi Anne Sheppeard is a first generation Christian and understands that building meaningful, life-valued traditions is a lot like building a bridge's foundation in a moving river. We must keep our eyes on Jesus. Contact: 700 E. Washington #230, Colton, CA 92324.

Penny Shoup was born on a farm in Ohio and currently lives in Columbia, TN, with her husband, Bruce. She worked as a Registered Nurse but is now home schooling her four children. Penny loves children, horses, dogs and, of course, writing. She just finished writing the novel, *In His Time*.

Patricia Smith is the director of P.A.S.S. Ministries (Practical Application of Scriptural Solutions). Her ability to punctuate Biblical truths with humor and realism make Patricia a desired speaker for women's functions across the country. She and her husband, "Smitty," have three daughters.

Debi Stack is a freelance editor, writer, co-author, ghostwriter, columnist, and marketing consultant who also speaks at writer's functions. Contact: P.O. Box 11805, Kansas City, MO 64138-0305. (816) 763-5743. StackEdits@aol.com.

BettyRuth Stevens started to write when twelve years old and won a contest in a children's radio program. Since then, she has published short stories, articles, and poems and turned professional in the '70's. BettyRuth is a member of several writers groups and the mother of two grown children.

Patty Stump enjoys speaking at women's retreats, marriage seminars, Bible studies and special church events. She is also a wife, Christian counselor, freelance writer, and full time mom to T.J. and Elisabeth. Contact: P. O. Box 5003, Glendale, AZ 85312. (602) 938-1460.

Nanette Thorsen-Snipes is the author of a small inspirational book and over 250 articles, short stories, and devotionals. She was 1994 "Writer of the Year" at the Georgia Christian Writers' Conference. Contact: 355 Pinecrest Terrace, Bufurd, GA 30518. (770) 945-3093.

Doris Hays Toppen is a freelance writer published in national magazines, creative writing teacher and speaker. She enjoys biking, hiking, and camping with her four children, five grandchildren and their families. She lives at the foot of Mt. Si in Washington. Contact: 502 Janet Ave., NE, North Bend, WA 98045. (206) 888-0372.

Gail Wenos is a humorist and member of the National Speakers Association, who speaks to a variety of audiences throughout the United States. Whether speaking to corporate audiences, associations, or churches, her programs are more than entertainment . . . they aim for the heart.

Jo White is a well-healed survivor of sexual/spiritual abuse and has formed and facilitated a support group for Christian women molested as children. She is currently writing a book for victims abused by Christians. Contact: 8083 Minstead Ave., Hesperia, CA 92345-7021. (619) 244-1186.

Sharon Wilkins is a speaker and an early childhood educator of 25 years. Her book, *Ready for Kindergarten*, helps parents and teachers prepare children for success. Sharon is married and has two daughters. Contact: 1157 W. Peninsula Dr., Gilbert, AZ 85233.